SPINOZA'S PANTHEISM

SPINOZA'S PANTHEISM

Shahin Soltanian

Kashfence Trust Publications

ISBN 978-0-473-53734-0 (paperback)

ISBN 978-0-473-53735-7 (kindle)

A catalogue record for this book is available from the National Library of New Zealand.

Published by Kashfence Trust Publications, Auckland

Contents

INTRODUCTION

During 17th century A.D Europe, the polemic discussions between the rationalists and empiricists were at their earliest and most critical stages. Both of the two distinct schools of thought were battling it out in order to gain supremacy among the ethical and moral worldviews and to identify in this field the role of God and God's so called appointed authority among the people. The arena of this confrontation was the field of epistemology. On the one hand, empiricism was claiming a degree of subjectivity for knowledge due to it being acquired through personal experience and on the other hand, the rationalists were asserting its objectivity due to innateness of many primary ideas. Descartes had just completed his reply to empiricism and scepticism and Cartesian thought was the dominant view. From among this conflict, excommunicated from the synagogue for being one of the proponents of Descartes, a new philosopher emerged claiming to have found a solution to the role of religion in ethics and morality. However, his battle ground was not the field of epistemology. His geometric style of discussion had aimed to shake the very foundation of theological schools of thought in Europe. He was treading a forbidden path. He was discussing the 'identity of God'. Benedictus De Spinoza, prior to any discussion about the human mind and his/her knowledge, *"started with God"*.

It could be said that Spinoza's *Ethics* was the book responsible for modern day pantheism in the west. The central theme of his *Ethics* and what he is widely famous for is his identification of, and the method of, identifying God with nature. According to Spinoza, God is not a separate entity to nature but one and the same. Spinoza's universe or world is not divided into two; he is not a proponent of a dual world where on the one side a creator, a personal God 'creates' all other existing entities while on the other side those existing entities subsist and are 'guided' by that creator. He proclaims such a view as opposed to rational deduction. Spinoza claims that if a person is truly to contemplate, rationally, about the world, they will ultimately come to the conclusion that such a world is not dual in 'nature' but only in the different way that this nature subsists. Hence, he divides nature into *natura naturans* and *natura naturata*, that is to say he divides it into 'active nature' and 'passive nature'. The former he labels *substance* and the latter he calls *modes*.[1]

The central theme of Spinoza's pantheism, namely, the idea of God and nature being one and the same entity will be the topic of discourse in this book. Hence, this dissertation will concentrate mainly on part one of Spinoza's *Ethics* titled 'Concerning God', although parts of the other sections will also be mentioned and discussed in order to clarify the different subjects discussed in part one.

Many authors have presented various different kinds of interpretation of Spinoza's view of God and nature. The current work differs with those

---

[1]Benedictus De Spinoza, *Ethics*, trans. A. Boyle (London: J.M. Dent & Sons Ltd), Part 1, Note for proposition XXIX, 24.

works in some respects. Other written works on Spinoza (some of which will be mentioned) seem to have simply expounded and attempted to improve the central themes in his philosophy.[2] However, if an essay simply expounds a certain philosophical outlook and adds on to that outlook without first establishing its soundness then that essay falls in danger of continuing an already fallacious argument. Hence, this essay will attempt to fulfil several goals.

First, Spinoza's world view will be evaluated without much reference to Cartesian or any other thought that was dominant in his time. Spinoza provides ample explanations in his geometric style of writing for a full understanding of his definitions of the various terms and his proofs for the various propositions. Second, a 'critical' evaluation of Spinoza's view is presented with the aim is to find out whether Spinoza's claims are sound (or rational). The result of that evaluation will decide whether or not his philosophy needs to be further improved. Third, the criticisms presented in this essay against Spinoza's philosophy will follow a rigid philosophical demonstration, untangling Spinoza's arguments and finally demonstrating its fallacies.

The discourse is divided into three sections. The first section concerns a discussion of Spinoza's reality. This section will include a description and analysis of how Spinoza categorizes reality, namely his division of reality into *substance, attribute and modes*, and how he relates to each other the elements that constitute his reality (i.e. Spinoza's God and nature

---

[2]Such as Stuart Hampshire in his book titled *Spinoza*, E. M. Curly in his book titled *Spinoza's Metaphysics: An Essay in Interpretation*, and Henry E. Allison in his book titled *Benedictus de Spinoza: An Introduction*.

relationship). The second section will include evaluation and criticisms of Spinoza's pantheism. Arguments will be put forward to demonstrate the fallacies that were contained in Spinoza's argument, beginning with criticism of his ontological arguments for the existence of God (or according to Spinoza, substance) and ending with the criticism of Spinoza's idea that a being whose existence is necessary can be one with a being whose existence is contingent. Some other features of Spinoza's pantheism will also be discussed in this section in order to see whether or not any part of Spinoza's pantheism can be rescued. Based on the criticisms provided in this section it will be shown that Spinoza's philosophy is untenable. In this section the relationship between an existential cause and its effects will be discussed and the theory of positive and negative attributes of existence will be introduced. In the third section a theory will be introduced from Islamic philosophy known as 'Unity of Existents', which although it does not claim to be pantheistic, it is a version of pantheism and very similar to Spinoza's philosophical theory. The theory of the unity of existents will be analysed and tested with the criticisms presented against Spinoza's philosophical arguments. It will be demonstrated that even though the idea of the unity of existence might not be subject to some of the criticisms that can be directed toward Spinoza's pantheism, it nevertheless is fallacious on the same fundamental grounds as that philosophical view.

1   SPINOZA'S REALITY

In accordance with the geometrical style of reasoning, Spinoza begins the first part of his *Ethics* defining the principal terms and axioms which he later uses in his demonstrations. These terms and axioms are elaborated on in his propositions and proofs.

 Spinoza defines reality using three main terms, namely, substance, attributes and modes, but he claims only two of these, namely substance and modes, have external reality while attributes on the other hand are mental conceptions or the limited understanding that human beings have of the essence of substance (these topics will be elaborated on further in the book). To better understand and as a result, better analyse Spinoza's pantheism it is vital that these terms are explicated in detail. The objects postulated for these terms are what constitute Spinoza's reality.

Substance and Attributes

It could be said that the most original definition of a concept introduced in the *Ethics*, is that of substance defined as something "which is in itself and is conceived through itself".[3] Of course, this was not the first time the term substance was introduced by a philosopher, but it was the first time

---

[3]Spinoza, "Ethics," Part 1, Definition III, 1.

that the term substance was given such a unique definition. It was unique not only because it describes substance as that which is in itself or exists through itself but also as that which is 'conceived' through itself. Spinoza proposed a logical necessity between existing through itself and being conceived through itself. Hence, something which exists through itself by logical necessity has to be conceived through itself. Attributes, for Spinoza was what the mind (or intellect) understands of the essence of substance.[4]

On the surface it might seem that Spinoza's definition of attribute is no different to that of Descartes, but at least to Spinoza himself there was a fundamental difference. While Descartes stated that the attributes of God produce the conception of the 'infinite substance of God' in the intellect, Spinoza stated that the 'infinite substance' can be conceived (and in fact has to be conceived) through itself, while the attributes are the intellect's understanding of the various immanent natures within the substance.[5] There will be more discussion on Spinoza's attributes below.

It is important to elaborate on what Spinoza means by something existing through itself. In the first definition of part one of *Ethics*[6], Spinoza states that something is said to be the cause of itself when it necessarily exists and its existence is included in its essence. Spinoza's argument in this regard relies on two consecutive premises, firstly that substance does not have a cause for its existence and secondly that substance

---

[4]Spinoza, "Ethics," Part 1, Definition IV, 1.

[5]Spinoza, "Ethics," Part 1, Definition IV, 1.

[6]Spinoza, "Ethics," Part 1, Definition I, 1.

'necessarily' exists.[7] With that in mind he sets out to prove that substance is the cause of itself.

Even though Spinoza, like other philosophers of his time, terms that which existence is included in its essence as 'self-caused', it is important not to confuse his terminology and claim that there is a contradiction in the idea of self-causation. That which existence is included in its essence, does not cause itself to exist in the sense that it did not exist then it caused itself to exist, since such a proposition would be absurd. Something which does not exist cannot bring itself into existence, it cannot give itself something which it does not have (i.e., it is contradictory to claim that something can give itself existence because it would be stating that it is and it is not existent at the same time). The argument that everything needs a cause for its existence and therefore something which does not have an external cause for its existence must be its own cause is simply flawed if considered in the aforementioned sense. However, the argument that every existent entity which is in need of another for its existence must have a cause for its existence, while that existent entity which is not in need of another for its existence does not need a cause for its existence is valid and sound. From such an argument it follows that the existing thing which is not in need of anything for its existence (i.e., it is independent in terms of its existence), includes existence in its essence.[8]

---

[7]It is obvious that his argument relies on these two premises because he states, "I Understand that to be Cause of Itself (causa sui) **whose essence involves existence** and **whose nature cannot be conceived unless existing**."

[8]One point has to be clarified. Consider the following argument: That existent entity which does not need another for its existence has always existed and

It seems that Spinoza's use of the term self-caused is simply keeping to the philosophical vernacularism of his time and what he really intended to describe through such a term was an entity whose reason for existing was not outside of itself. An entity that exists solely because of itself does not have a cause for its existence. Spinoza himself hints to this point in his proof for proposition seven of part one of the *Ethics* when he states:

> A substance cannot be produced from anything else (prev. Prop., Coroll.): it will therefore be its own cause, **that is** (Def. I) **its essence necessarily involves existence, or existence appertains to the nature of it.**[9]

That which its essence necessarily involves existence does not have a cause for its existence as it was never the case that it did not exist.

therefore has never brought itself into existence. This argument does not mean that the proof for it not needing another for its existence is the fact that it has always existed. A claim cannot be put forward that everything which has always existed must exist necessarily. Something which has always existed in the temporal sense could have always existed because it has been receiving its existence from another being (say, a necessarily existing being for example). Timelessness, in the sense that it is free from the limitations of time, is just a logical necessity for that existent entity which does not need another entity for its existence. That existent entity which does not need another for its existence could not have at one time not existed (i.e., it could not be temporal), because then its coming into existence means that it would have been brought into existence by another. Its need for another for its coming into existence is the result of it not having existence. Since it did not have existence it could not have given existence to itself. If it could not give itself existence but it began to exist then it must have been given existence or made existent by another. In this sense all temporal entities therefore must have a cause for their existence. However, the conclusion that follows from the argument given in the text (i.e., that every existent entity which is in need of another for its existence must have a cause for its existence, while that existent entity which is not in need of another for its existence does not need a cause for its existence) is that everything which is in need of another for its existence, whether it has always existed or not, needs a cause for its existence.

[9]Spinoza, "Ethics," Part 1, Proof for proposition VII, 4.

Spinoza's proof (proposition one to seven of part one) for why a substance does not need a cause for its existence seems to consist of the argument that substances which have distinct attributes to one another cannot be the cause of each other. According to Spinoza, things can be distinguished from one another either through their attributes or their modifications. Modification can also be termed as an effect, since Spinoza believed modifications are effects of substance. Hence, for Spinoza, things can be distinguished from each other either through their attributes or their effects. Since, to Spinoza, it is absurd to distinguish between substances through things that are existentially dependent on them (or are existentially after substances), then distinction cannot be made between substances through their modifications and can only be made through their attributes.[10]

A note should be added here that the reason why Spinoza would not accept modifications of substance as an indication of the distinction between two or more substances is due to the causal relationship which he postulates between substance and modes. To Spinoza, effects are understood through their cause.[11] Hence, before the effects are understood the causes have to be understood. Substance in the Spinozistic sense causally precedes modes because modes are effects of substance. Hence, before modes and their distinction are recognised,

---

[10]The statement made by Spinoza in the proof of proposition five of part one, "...since a substance is prior in its nature to its modification, therefore let modification be laid aside..." seems to indicate that by prior in nature, Spinoza is hinting at the existential dependence of modification on substance or even at the existence of substance being prior to that of modification.

[11]Spinoza, "Ethics," Part 1, Axiom IV, 2.

substances and any distinction between them have to be understood first. If it has not been established that there is more than one substance then the plurality of modes is not an indication that there can be several substances, since it could be the case that they are the effect of only one substance.[12]

Spinoza proceeds with his argument for why a substance does not have a cause for its existence by stating that two substances which have distinct attribute/s have nothing in common with each other. He asserts that since a substance has an attribute or a set of attributes that cannot be found in any other substance then the former substance has to be conceived through itself (since it is the only thing with those attributes). Therefore, because the conception of a substance does not depend on any other, then it does not have anything in common with any other. In addition, since each substance can only be conceived through itself and no other, then, according to Spinoza, it follows that substances cannot be the cause of each other.

Spinoza also gives the argument stated above using a more conventional method in proposition six, by stating that a substance cannot give what it does not have. In other words, if a substance lacks a certain attribute then it cannot be the existential cause of producing something which will have that attribute.

Furthermore, Spinoza rules out the idea of there being several existing substances with identical attributes. If two substances have identical

---

[12]Spinoza, "Ethics," Part 1, Note for the proof of proposition X, 7.

attributes (in every way) then one cannot be distinguished from the other (since substances can only be distinguished from each other through their attributes) and if there is no distinction between them then they are one and the same thing and there is no 'them/they'.[13]

Spinoza's proof for why substance necessarily 'exists' can be found further into part one in proposition eleven where he reasons for substance's existence through three versions of the ontological argument, two of which are his own uniquely constructed arguments and one of which is a common version of the ontological argument. For the purpose of this book, only the two arguments unique to Spinoza will be considered.

For his first argument Spinoza states:

If you deny it, conceive, if it be possible, that God does not exist. Then (Ax. 7) his essence does not involve existence. But this (Prop. 7) is absurd. Therefore God necessarily exists.[14]

There is little that can be added to what Spinoza has already stated because the argument he presents is clear. The argument is a repeat of the ontological argument that was presented by Descartes,[15] except modified in order to present it in a demonstrative form. Spinoza had (supposedly) already proved in proposition seven that what he terms God

---

[13]Spinoza, "Ethics," Part 1, Proposition VI and XIV, 11.

[14]Spinoza, "Ethics," Part 1, First proof for proposition XI, 8.

[15]Benedictus Spinoza, *The Principles of Descartes Philosophy* (Illinois: Open Court, 1974), 30-31.

or substance involves existence in its essence.[16]   In his ontological argument Spinoza states that if God's 'non-existence' is asserted then it has to also be accepted that his essence does not include existence. However, according to proposition seven, substance (which for Spinoza is God) does include existence in its essence. Hence, to state that substance does not exist would be the same as stating that an entity that includes existence in its essence does not include existence in its essence (or includes non-existence in its essence). Such a proposition would be a conjunction of contradictories and absurd. Therefore, it can never be asserted that substance does not exist, which means that substance exists necessarily. Spinoza's aforementioned argument can also be put into a syllogistic form in order to better clarify his position. Hence, his argument would read as follows:

Premise 1.   That which includes existence in its essence is the same as that which does not accept non-existence in its essence.

Premise 2. (hidden premise)   That which does not accept non-existence in its essence is that which necessarily exists.

Premise 3.   Therefore that which includes existence in its essence is that which exists necessarily.

The second ontological argument Spinoza presents for the necessary existence of substance is more perplexing than the first and hence it has

---

[16]Spinoza, "Ethics," Part 1, Proposition VII, 4.

been avoided by some interpreters of *Ethics*.   The reason for this perplexity is mostly due to some of the notions of causality that Spinoza uses as premise for this argument while he does not anywhere in *Ethics* attempt to elaborate on them.

Spinoza states that a cause must be assigned to why a thing exists or does not exist. Such a cause is either from within the thing or external to it. According to Spinoza, when concepts are assessed with existence they can be categorised in three different ways:

1)   It is impossible for something to exist.
2)   It is possible for something to either exist or not to exist.
3)   It is necessary for something to exist.

The cause for why it is impossible for a concept to exist is within the nature of things themselves. Spinoza gives the example of a circle and states that it is within the nature of a circle (or more accurately what he means is a circular object) not to accept the property of being square as a predicate, therefore the cause of the non-existence of a square-circle is the nature of circle (or circular object) itself. By this argument Spinoza seems to be asserting that the impossibility of a concept existing in reality depends on an already existing thing. Hence, for it to be impossible for a square-circle to exist there has to be a circle that exists in the first place. This interpretation of Spinoza's statement is confirmed when he presents one of his proofs for the necessary existence of substance (which will be discussed below). However, if such a definition of an impossible object is accepted then it will not be the case that an impossible object such as a square circle cannot exist. If there is no circle to begin with, that is to say if there is no circle or square, then instead of a circle being created first or a square being created first, a square-circle is created then it should be possible for that object (i.e. a square-circle) to exist. This will be further elaborated on in the second section when Spinoza's theory is critically analysed.

Even though there is a problem with Spinoza's definition of why an impossible object does not exist, nevertheless it can be overlooked while still retaining Spinoza's main pantheistic theory. However, it had to be mentioned because Spinoza relies on this definition as one of the reasons for why an object does not exist and tries to use it to prove the necessary existence of substance.[17]

Spinoza also states that there are entities which when assessed with existence it is possible for them to both exist and not exist. Hence, it cannot be impossible for them to exist nor is it necessary for them to exist.[18] According to Spinoza, the cause for existence and non-existence of beings which existence is possible for them but not necessary is not

---

[17]There is actually no need for Spinoza to have made such an argument as it is enough and in fact more accurate to state that since circularity and squareness are contradictory to each other they cannot be instantiated in the same thing. However, Spinoza's argument provides him with a convenient rationale which he uses to prove the existence of substance.

[18]For further elaboration consider the following: if it is impossible for something to exist then it cannot be possible for it to exist as is apparent from the word 'impossible'. Also, if something which has necessary existence in the sense that it is existent and its essence includes existence (existence is predicated to its essence) then it cannot be the case it could not exist. If it was the case that something which has necessary existence could not exist then existence is not necessary for it and that is a contradiction.

from within themselves and for that reason they need an external entity to make them existent and non-existent, which is also the reason why existence is neither necessary nor impossible for them. For example, the reason why a circle (or circular object) exists or does not exist is due to the "universal order of corporeal nature" and not the nature of a circle.

The third of the above mentioned categories of concepts includes that which it is not possible for it not to exist, that is to say that which has necessary existence or exists necessarily. Spinoza asserts that since existence is predicated to the essence of substance then the cause for the existence of substance is within the substance itself. Therefore existence is necessary for the substance.

It seems that the argument should really need no further elaboration as it is identical to his first proof, but Spinoza does not stop there and he actually includes another independent argument within the aforementioned argument. He states that since the cause for a thing's non-existence has to be from within it, then to assert substance's non-existence would be to admit to the existence of substance.[19] It seems that what Spinoza is arguing for is that since substance can only be known through itself then there is no other concept included in its definition except substance itself. Hence, to state that there is something included in the concept of substance which is the cause of the substance's non-existence is simply stating that it is substance that is preventing substance from existing (hence existence of substance being admitted) and that

---

[19]Spinoza uses the term God instead of substance at this point of his argument.

would be admitting to the existence and non-existence of substance at the same time, which is an obvious contradiction.

Spinoza also takes into consideration the argument that the cause for the substance's non-existence could be from other than itself. According to Spinoza, in such a case that other has to be either of the same nature (in which case substance's existence is affirmed) or of different nature. However, if the other is different in nature then it cannot be the cause for the existence or non-existence of the substance. Hence, Spinoza concludes from his second ontological argument for the existence of substance that a being that is absolutely perfect in every way and which does not have a cause for its existence and non-existence from without or within must by necessity exist.

By providing his evidence that substance includes existence in its essence and that it necessarily exists, Spinoza reaches the conclusion that substance does not need a cause for its existence.

Previously it was mentioned that, for Spinoza, attributes are not qualities which lead to the conception of substance and in fact they are the intellect's understanding of the various natural qualities inherent in the essence of the substance.[20] It is important to understand what Spinoza means when he gives attributes such a definition, because, even though attributes for Spinoza do not have existence outside of the mind,[21]

---

[20]Spinoza, "Ethics," Part 1, Proof of Proposition X, 7.

[21]Spinoza scholars are divided on the nature of attributes; some stating that for Spinoza attributes have existence outside of the intellect. However, the text of *Ethics* seems to indicate that for Spinoza attributes are the different ways that the intellect can perceive the nature of substance. E.M. Curley points out in this

they nevertheless do link substance with its effects (i.e. Modes). Hence, to have a better understanding of Spinoza's definition of the attributes of substance would ultimately aid in the understanding of the link between substance and modes, which is the core of Spinoza's Pantheism.

In part one of *Ethics*, in definition four Spinoza describes an attribute as:

> ...that which the intellect perceives as constituting the essence of substance.

In the same part in proposition nine, Spinoza states that because attributes are the mind's understanding of what constitutes the essence of a substance then if a substance has more reality it would mean that it has more attributes. Since substance is infinite then it logically follows that it has infinite attributes.[22]

Spinoza attempts to prove the infiniteness and indivisibility of substance using the arguments he presented for why one substance cannot cause the existence of another substance and that there cannot exist two or more identical substances. Something is finite (according to Spinoza) if it is limited by another with the same nature, which in the case of substance would be another substance with the same attributes, but since it is

---

regard that in *Epistolae,* Spinoza specifically asserts that the two terms (i.e., substance and attribute) refer to the same thing. Curley further notes that Spinoza mentions the two names Israel and Jacob as an example of how two terms could refer to the one and the same thing (i.e., both Israel and Jacob refer to the same person). See: E.M. Curley, *Spinoza's Metaphysics: An Essay in Interpretation* (Massachusetts: Harvard University Press, 1969), p.17.

[22]Spinoza, "Ethics," Part 1, Proposition XI, 7.

impossible for two or more substances to exist with the same attributes then it must be the case that substance is infinite.[23]

Similarly, Spinoza asserts that if substance is divisible, then either the parts will have the same attributes (or nature) as the whole or they will not. In the former case (i.e. the parts of the substance have the same attribute as the whole of the substance) it would follow that more than one substance with the same attributes exists and that is against the proof given for the impossibility of two or more substances existing with the same attributes (as discussed above).[24]   In terms of the latter proposition, that is to say if it was the case that the parts of substance do not have the same attributes (or nature) as substance itself or have only one of its attributes, it follows that substance does not have reality in itself and is simply an aggregate of the different parts. Such a proposition would lead to the claim that a necessarily existing substance which is absolutely infinite and has existence included in its essence would no longer exist and that is a contradiction in terms.[25]

Spinoza also presents another argument for why substance is indivisible. The conception of substance, according to Spinoza, includes only substance. Hence, part of a substance would also be substance. But then such a proposition would mean that substance is both an infinite whole and a finite part and that is absurd. Therefore substance is indivisible.[26]

---

[23]Spinoza, "Ethics," Part 1, Proposition VIII, 4.

[24]Spinoza, "Ethics," Part 1, Proposition XII and XIII, 10.

[25]Spinoza, "Ethics," Part 1, Proposition XII and XIII, 10.

[26]Spinoza, "Ethics," Part 1, Note for Proposition XIII, 4.

The idea of substance having infinite attributes raises another question for Spinoza, which is, how is it that the one substance can have many attributes? For Spinoza this question relates back to the discussion of whether there can be more than one substance. An attribute is conceived without the need for another attribute (they are conceived through themselves) and since it is the intellect's abstraction of the natural qualities of the essence of substance, it could be claimed that different attributes express different essences (i.e. different substances). Spinoza seems to deal with this problem superficially and inadequately. In the note provided for proposition ten in part one, Spinoza states that because attributes are the mind's abstraction of the essence of substance (or at least some of its qualities) then it is quite natural for it to be conceived through itself since it is the property of the essence of substance to be conceived through itself. The proofs for why these attributes do not express different substances, Spinoza states, are those arguments he puts forward for the oneness, infiniteness and indivisibility of substance.[27]

Spinoza also presents a brief yet concise argument for the eternity of substance. Spinoza asserts that after proving that substance exists necessarily, eternity becomes an inevitable consequence (i.e. substance has always existed). If there has never been a time which substance did

---

[27] Spinoza needs to demonstrate how it is that two attributes, each of which is conceived through itself, does not represent a separate substance. To refer the reader to the proofs for the oneness, infinity and indivisibility of substance is begging the question since, those proofs require the assumption that all attributes belong to the one substance (as it will be discussed later).

not exist and it is impossible for there to be a time that substance would not exist, then it must be the case that substance is eternal.[28]

After proving that substance is eternal Spinoza goes on to prove that its essence is also eternal and does not change. Spinoza believes that since attributes are the mind's abstraction of the nature of the essence of substance, then if substance is eternal it follows that the attributes are also eternal. In addition, since attributes express substance's existence then it can be inferred that they express both the substance's essence and its existence. Because substance's essence and existence is expressed by one and the same thing in the intellect, that is to say attributes, then it follows that both the essence and the attribute is one and the same thing and hence both are eternal.[29]

Even though the major criticisms of Spinoza's pantheism will be discussed in section two of this essay, a brief note should be made about the aforementioned proof for why substance's essence is eternal. When it is proved that existence is included in the essence of an entity (what Spinoza believed to have proved) then there is no need to further argue for the essence and existence of that entity being one and the same thing. Hence, when it is proved that an entity's existence is eternal, it is automatically proved that its essence is eternal. The essence and existence of an entity in reality would ultimately be one and the same thing because if they were different then it could not be said that the essence of an existent entity is 'the essence' of the existent entity.

[28]Spinoza, "Ethics," Part 1, Proposition XIX, 18.

[29]Spinoza, "Ethics," Part 1, Proposition XX, 19.

Therefore Spinoza's argument for why God's (which for Spinoza is the same as substance) existence is one with his essence is really not required. Besides, his argument begs the question. Spinoza states that attributes express both the existence and essence of 'a' substance. By stating that there is 'an' entity that has existence and essence, it is already been assumed that both existence and essence is united in that entity (the word 'an' represents a unity). Therefore it cannot be argued back to that unity from the attributes of that entity when that unity has already been assumed. Spinoza also assumes this unity when he asserts that since attributes express substance's existence then they must also express substance's essence.

Nevertheless, the aforementioned argument is interesting in one respect, namely Spinoza's definition of what it means for substance to be eternal. In the first corollary of that argument, Spinoza states that if the essence and existence of substance is one and the same, then since the essence of substance is eternal so is the existence of substance. The notion of "eternal" for Spinoza does not mean duration with no beginning or end. What Spinoza really means by eternal is that it could never be the case that it could not exist, a notion which he provided proof for in his argument for why substance exists necessarily.[30] In the second corollary Spinoza states that because the essence and existence of the substance are one and the same and eternal (it is never the case that it does not exist) then it also follows that substance and all its attributes are immutable.[31]

---

[30]Spinoza, "Ethics," Part 1, corollary 1 of Proposition XX, 19.

Modes

Rocks, trees, human beings (both their intellect[32] and their corporeal body) and other finite things are what constitute Spinoza's *modes*. Spinoza does not concentrate as much on defining modes as he does defining the mode's relationship with substance. One reason for this approach could be due to the fact that humans, being contingent[33] beings themselves, are already acquainted with contingent beings, hence when a philosophical enquiry is made into the reason for the existence of the world, a reason is sought for how contingent beings (which Spinoza calls modes) have come into existence. This enquiry leads to an entity which is not contingent and is necessary and therefore this Necessary Being and its relationship with contingent beings becomes the main topic of discussion. Spinoza's notion of substance aimed to fill the position of the necessary entity. There is however certain characteristics of mode which can be mentioned independent of the discussion of its relationship with substance.

---

[31]Spinoza, "Ethics," Part 1, corollary 2 of Proposition XX, 19.

[32]Spinoza, "Ethics," Part 2, Proposition I, 38-39.

[33]The term contingent is used in this essay to mean that which does not include existence in its essence and is dependent on another being for its existence. Spinoza uses this definition for what he terms *natura naturata* or modifications, however he does not call them contingent. This issue will be taken up below and it will be shown why it is justified to call such entities contingent despite Spinoza's different use of the terminology. Nevertheless, it makes no difference whether the 'word' contingent is used or not because the definition given to the word contingent in this essay includes Spinoza's modifications.

Modes for Spinoza are effects of substance. Spinoza's definition of causality is a peculiar one in the sense that he proposes a correspondence between the casual relationship of two entities and their conceptions. For Spinoza, an effect is known through the conception of its cause.[34] Hence, because modes are the effects of substance, they are conceived through the conception of substance which in contrast with modes is conceived through itself.[35] Furthermore, because the cause for the existence of mode is not from within itself then it must be the case that the essence of mode does not contain (i.e., imply) existence.[36]

The last proposition (i.e. that the essence of mode does not include existence) is particularly important because it is used by Spinoza to deduce another significant aspect of his pantheism, that is to say the proposition that the mode is completely dependent on substance for its existence. The kind of dependency that Spinoza is proposing is not that of a creator which creates and then leaves the creation to its own accords. Spinoza puts forward an argument to prove that modes are not only brought into existence by substance but also they continually are in need of substance for their continued existence (that is, their sustenance).

---

[34]Spinoza, "Ethics," Part 1, axiom IV, p.2. Such a notion that an effect has to be conceived through its cause is untenable because it could be the case that a person knows that a ball was thrown but not know who it was thrown by. Besides, the very fact that some people reject the existence of substance yet they conceive the world, proves that they do not need to conceive of the substance in order to conceive the world.

[35]Spinoza, "Ethics," Part 1, Definition III and V and axiom IV, pp.1-2.

[36]Spinoza, "Ethics," Part 1, Proposition XXIV, 21.

Spinoza states in the proof and corollary of proposition twenty four of part one:

> For that whose nature (considered in itself) involves existence is its own cause and exists merely by necessity of its own nature...For whether things exist or whether they do not, however often we consider their essences, we will find it to involve neither existence or their duration, but only God to whose nature alone existence appertains.[37]

Spinoza seems to be arguing in this proposition that besides substance (which he has labelled God in this passage) no other existent thing has necessary existence.   The proof for this proposition is what was mentioned before for the impossibility of more than one substance existing (substance being the only necessary being).   Hence, the essence of modes (as mentioned in section one) do not include existence, which is why it is possible for them not to exist.[38]   In addition, the essences of modes can never include existence because whenever they are considered in relation to existence it is the case that their essences do not involve existence.   Therefore since the essences of modes can never include existence of and by themselves then it must be the case that

---

[37]Spinoza, "Ethics," Part 1, Proof and corollary of proposition XXIV, 21.

[38]There is a passage in *Ethics* which reads, "**For Whether things exist or whether they do not**, however often we consider their essence, we will find it to involve neither existence nor duration; and their essences cannot be the cause either of their existence or their duration, but only God, to whose nature alone existence appertains." This passage seems to indicate that Spinoza believes that entities the essences of which do not include existence can either exist or not exist (i.e., it is possible for them to exist or not to exist). Spinoza, "Ethics," Part 1, Corollary for proposition XXIV, 21.

something other than their essences has given them existence and continues to sustain their existence.

Further in proposition twenty five, Spinoza states that it is not only the existence of things that are caused by substance but also their essences, because if it was the case that the essences of things were not caused by substance then it would be the case that their essences can be conceived by other than substance, which means their existence is caused by other than substance. If the existence of essences of modes is not caused by substance then either those essences have necessary existence or they were caused by something other than substance, both claims which Spinoza regards as impossible.

Even though Spinoza states that modes have possible existence and not a necessary one (i.e. their essence does not include existence), he does not on the other hand consider them as 'contingent' - a distinction which seems to be unique to Spinoza's philosophy. Modes for Spinoza have a sort of necessity while contingent beings have no necessity whatsoever. The necessity of modes is due to their existence being determined by and dependent on substance. Off course, this does not mean that they have necessary existence in terms of existence being included in their essence, but that they are necessarily 'determined' to exist in a particular way. According to Spinoza, the existence and action of things are either determined by themselves or by substance. The existence and actions of modes cannot be determined by themselves because they do not have existence from themselves and exist only through substance (which has necessary existence).[39] Hence, it follows that the existence of the modes and the way they exist or act are determined by substance.

Substance exists necessarily and that for Spinoza also means that substance causes necessarily (in the sense that what substance causes is necessarily how such a thing had to be caused to exist). Modes are effects of substance and therefore their existence is determined necessarily. What Spinoza means by substance determining the existence and the action of something by necessity will be further discussed below when the relationship between modes and substances are considered. On the other hand, it would be appropriate to point out that the notion of contingency, according to how Spinoza describes it, is merely an illusion and in reality it is impossible for something to be contingent.[40]

Spinoza's God and Nature Relationship

As it is apparent from the title, the main aim of the current book is to evaluate and critique Spinoza's pantheism. Hence, the previous section was only a pedestal for providing enough explanation of the various components in Spinoza's pantheistic philosophy in order to better analyse the relationship between those components. A good starting point for

---

[39]Actions (or performances) are also caused by substance because the actions of modes, like them, do not exist by themselves and hence are in need of substance for their existence.

[40]Spinoza, "Ethics," Part 2, Proposition XLIV and Corollary, 71.

the discussion of Spinoza's pantheism is his distinction between substance and modes as active and passive nature.

Spinoza's substance has a double nature. The nature of substance which is conceived through itself, self-caused, immutable, infinite and eternal is the active nature (*natura naturans*).[41] On the other hand, the nature of substance which is caused to exist by substance, its conception depends on substance and is dependent on the substance for its continued existence is the passive nature (*natura naturata*).[42]

Spinoza's reality includes 'only' an infinite, indivisible and eternal substance with infinite and indivisible attributes that are modified in infinitely different ways.[43] Substance is an infinite and perfect being and therefore has ultimate reality. The more being an entity has the more attributes it has and substance which is infinite has infinite attributes.[44] Each of the infinite attributes of the substance expresses one of substance's qualities or natures and therefore each attribute is in itself infinite. However, attributes are not an entity separate to the substance and in fact they are not any type of entity at all, they are simply the intellect's understanding of the essence of the substance. In reality outside the mind (or the intellect) attributes are indivisible and one with

---

[41]Spinoza, "Ethics," Part 1, Note for proof of proposition XXIX, 24.

[42]Spinoza, "Ethics," Part 1, Note for proof of proposition XXIX, 24. For Spinoza's explanation about why *natura naturata* depends on substance for its existence see: Spinoza, "Ethics," Part 1, Proposition XXIV, 21.

[43]Spinoza, "Ethics," Part 1, Proposition XXX, 24.

[44]Spinoza, "Ethics," Part 1, Note for the proof of proposition XVI, 22.

the substance because the attributes simply represent the existence of substance. It is only in the realm of the limited mind that attributes are abstracted from the essence of an indivisible substance.

> AN ATTRIBUTE (attributum) I understand to be **that which the intellect perceives** as constituting the essence of a substance[45]...An attribute **is that which the intellect perceives** of a substance constituting its essence[46]...

Among the infinite attributes of active nature is the attribute of thought and extension.[47]   The attribute of extension cannot be denied from substance as that would mean that substance is finite and not a perfect being, for a perfect being has all the conceivable attributes. Besides, such a claim would purport another substance because extension cannot come from a substance that does not have extension itself.[48] Objects such as rocks, trees and animal and human bodies are only a limited representation of the infinite modification (namely corporeality) of the attribute of extension. Individual human intellects are also a limited representation of an infinite mode, but not that of corporeality but rather that of intellect which is the representation of the attribute of thought.[49]

---

[45]Spinoza, "Ethics," Part 1, Definition IV, 1.

[46]Spinoza, "Ethics," Part 1, Proof for proposition X, 7.

[47]Spinoza, "Ethics," Part 2, Proposition I, 38-39; Spinoza, "Ethics," Part 2, Proposition II, 39.

[48]Spinoza, "Ethics," Part 1, Note for proof of proposition XV, 11-15.

[49]Spinoza, "Ethics," Part 2, Proposition I, 38-39.

Hence, in a sense, attributes that the mind abstracts from the essence of the substance is the mind's finite understanding of the infinite substance.

> The formal being of ideas is a mode of thinking (as is self evident), that is (coroll, prop. 25, part I.), a mode which expresses in a certain manner the nature of God in so far as he is a thinking thing, and therefore (prop. 10, Part I.) involves the conception of no other attribute of God, ...[50]

Each attribute is manifested through its modification. It is important to clarify what Spinoza means by asserting that each attribute of substance is manifested through its modifications. Quite often Spinoza's assertion is taken to mean that attributes are intermediate causes between substance and modification; however this is an incorrect interpretation of Spinoza. As it was already mentioned, attributes, for Spinoza, seem to be only the intellect's limited understanding of the substance's essence and in reality all the attributes of substance are actually one with the substance. Hence, when Spinoza claims that each attribute is manifested through its modifications, he does not seem to be claiming that attributes have existence external to the mind; he seems to be asserting that the various different modifications of 'substance' represents a different attribute of it. Modification which follows from an attribute is infinite because attributes being a representation of the essence of substance are infinite.[51] Furthermore, modification that follows from the first modification of attributes is also infinite.[52]   Hence, there is a series of infinite

---

[50]Spinoza, "Ethics," Part 2, Proposition V, 40.

[51]Spinoza, "Ethics," Part 1, Proposition XXI, 19.

modifications which follow one after the other from the infinite attribute of substance. On the surface it might seem that all other modifications but the first are independent of the substance but this is not the case. Even though, for example, the second modification is caused by the first modification and hence dependent on the first modification for its existence, nevertheless, it is ultimately dependent on the substance because the existence of the first modification is dependent on the substance. If the first modification did not exist then the second would not exist either. Therefore these modifications are all dependent on the substance for their existence and their proximity does not reduce their dependence.[53]

Infinite modifications are caused by infinite modifications and finite modifications follow from finite modification.[54] Finite modification is only the mind's understanding of infinite modification as in reality modification is infinite and not divided.

> Thence if any wish to consider the matter rightly, they will see that
> all absurdities..., from which they wish to conclude that extended
> substance is finite, follow not from the fact that an infinite quantity
> is supposed, but that they suppose an infinite quantity to be
> measurable and composed of finite part. But this is the same as we
> have shown in proposition 12;...For corporeal substance, which can

---

[52]Spinoza, "Ethics," Part 1, Proposition XXII and XXIII, 20.

[53]Spinoza, "Ethics," Part 1, Note for proof of proposition XXVIII, 23.

[54] Spinoza, "Ethics," Part 1, Proposition XXII and XXIII, 20; Spinoza, "Ethics," Part 1, Proposition XXVIII, 22.

only be conceived as infinite, without like and indivisible, they conceive, in order to prove it finite, to be composed of finite parts and to be multiplex and divisible. Thus also others having pretended that a line is composed of points, can find many arguments[55] wherewith to show that a line cannot be infinitely divided.[56]

Modifications exist in substance and the proof for this is that they are dependent on the substance for their existence. Because all modification is dependent on substance for their existence then it is the case that they cannot be conceived or exist without substance. Because they cannot be conceived or exist without substance then it must be the case that they exist within substance.[57] Substance, therefore, is the cause of things that are within it. That is to say it is the immanent cause of things and not the transient cause. The proposition that things exist within substance is further strengthened by the proposition that more than one substance cannot exist. If things did not exist within substance then they would be substances themselves and that, according to Spinoza, is an impossible assertion.[58]

Human beings are aggregates of only finite modes, part of the infinite modifications of the infinite ways substance can be modified. They are finite modifications of those qualities of substance which is known

[55]Probably referring to such arguments as Zeno's paradox.

[56]Spinoza, "Ethics," Part 1, Note for proof of proposition XV, 13.

[57]Spinoza, "Ethics," Part 1, Proposition XV, 11-15.

[58]Spinoza, "Ethics," Part 1, Proposition XVIII, 18.

through the mind as the attribute of thought and extension. Hence, human beings can only perceive these two attributes (i.e., thought and extension) out of the infinite attributes that constitute the essence of substance.[59]

Modes are determined to exist and act by the substance. Hence, the existence and actions of modes have been determined and there is no alteration of this action. The existence and actions of modes were determined by substance by necessity and not by choice, that is to say that substance did not choose to cause the existence and action of modes as they are but it was by necessity that substance caused them.[60]

It is from the power of the substance that all modifications follow. But this power is not separate to the active nature, for it is from the same power which the active nature's essence and all that follows from its essence exist.[61] In addition, because the power of substance is not separate to the substance then it must exist necessarily like substance.[62]

It is important to note that for Spinoza the power of substance (or God) is not limited to a single attribute, such as the attribute of thought for example. Hence, Spinoza believes that each of the attributes that express substance's power is manifested, individually, without the need for

---

[59]Spinoza, "Ethics," Part 2, Corollary of proposition X and corollary of proposition XI, 44-46.

[60]Spinoza, "Ethics," Part 1, Proposition XXXII, 25.

[61]Spinoza, "Ethics," Part 1, Proposition XXXIV, 29.

[62]Spinoza, "Ethics," Part 1, Proposition XXXV, 29.

intermediate attributes.[63] Consequently, Spinoza does not put forward a causal relationship based on the contemplating action of the One, like those of some Neo-Platonists and emanationist philosophers. Some Neo-Platonist and emanationist philosophers before (and even after) Spinoza, such as Plotinus[64], had suggested the intermediary of an intellectual entity (which Plotinus labels *The Intelligence*), between the Ultimate One and the multiplicity of its emanation.[65] For Spinoza on the other hand, thought (the modification of which is intellect) is not an attribute that ranks above other attributes (such as the attribute of extension for example). Spinoza places the attribute of thought 'alongside' other attributes, stating that all attributes are infinite and represent the infinite essence of substance. Hence, the power of substance is represented by infinite attributes.

However, there is one important aspect of Spinoza's philosophy that corresponds with Plotinus's theory of emanation, namely, the union between God's (substance according to Spinoza) infinite power of acting and His infinite power of thinking. According to Plotinus the first being that emanates from the One is known as the Intellegence (*Nous*). *Nous* exists due to nothing more than the One knowing itself. Other existents then follow from *Nous* due to the contemplating action of the Nous, and so on.[66] Similarly, Spinoza also claims the union of thought and action in

---

[63]Spinoza, "Ethics," Part 2, Proof and corollary for proposition VI, 41.

[64]Plotinus – A Greek Philosopher, born in Egypt and lived around 204 to 270 C.E. He is most famous for being the founder of Neo-Platonism.

[65]Moore, Edward. 'Plotinus (204-270 C.E.)', The Internet Encyclopedia of Philosophy, <http://www.iep.utm.edu/p/plotinus.htm> (2004)

substance. God's power of thinking, according to Spinoza, is the same as his power of acting and therefore, for substance to cause the existence of modes is the same as it thinking about those modes.[67] By asserting a union between God's power of thinking and His action, Spinoza elaborates on what he means by substance being the cause of modifications within itself.

As it has already been stated, for Spinoza modes exist within the substance and they are modifications of substance. Consequently, the corporeality of a corporeal object is the modification of the attribute of extension. In the same way, the idea of that corporeal object is also a modification of the attribute of thought. Because in reality all of substance's modifications are existentially one with the substance, then it follows that in reality the idea of a corporeal object is one with its corporeality and they both exist within the substance. Hence, when substance has the idea of a corporeal object within it (i.e., knows the corporeal object), then it also has the extension of the corporeal object within it. In this way substance is the cause of the modifications within it. [68]

Hence, for Spinoza, in reality there exists only one substance but with infinite attributes each of which have infinite modifications. This reality is only divided into many levels of existence when it is considered by an

---

[66]Spinoza, "Ethics," Part 2, Proof and corollary for proposition VI, 41.

[67]Spinoza, "Ethics," Part 2, Corollary and note for proposition VII, 41-42.

[68] Spinoza, "Ethics," Part 2, Note for proposition VII, 41-42.

entity which is only a limited representation of this whole and therefore perceives only a limited representation of this whole.

It is important to also discuss how Spinoza comes to the conclusion that the modes of substance exist within the substance and are one with the substance rather than existing separate to the substance. For Spinoza, there cannot be more than one substance, which means that there is only one substance that exists in reality; everything else is modes of substance. However, modes cannot exist by themselves and are dependent on the substance for their existence (both origin and continued existence). Spinoza concludes that since modes are dependent on substance for their existence then they must be one with the substance, in terms of existing within the substance. Spinoza himself does not elaborate on his assertion that existential dependence is also existential unity.

What followed was Spinoza's view of reality, a view that is commonly labelled pantheism. Spinoza wrote the *Ethics* in order to clarify his pantheistic philosophy. From his definitions and axioms he carefully constructed the propositions that constituted his outlook of the world. Spinoza's pantheism has been the subject of many commentaries and it has inspired many to develop their own pantheistic views of the world. However, there is a fundamental contradiction entailed in such a theory that renders it untenable. This contradiction can be found in other pantheistic theories as well and it is so fundamental that despite being more advanced in regards to some of their other aspects, are nevertheless, still untenable. The aforementioned contradiction is the idea that contingent beings can 'be' or 'be united' with the Necessary

Being. The next section is dedicated to the demonstration of this contradiction in addition to the analysis of some of the other issues which are unique to Spinoza's pantheistic philosophy.

2   EVALUATION AND CRITICISM

There are various ways in which Spinoza's pantheism can be criticized because his theory has major flaws both on grounds of validity of his arguments (because he seems to beg the question in many places) and in terms of soundness of his arguments. On the other hand, it has to also be taken into account that there are some criticisms which apply to Spinoza's theory only and not pantheism in general. Some of the flaws in his theory can be overcome with arguments that were not available to Spinoza. Hence, the criticisms towards Spinoza's pantheism will be divided into two sub-sections. The first part will deal with the main principles upon which Spinoza's pantheism is constructed. The second part will deal with the fundamental contradiction in Spinoza's criticism which cannot be overcome even by more sophisticated pantheistic theories.

Principles of Spinoza's Pantheism

The notion of self-causality (which as it was mentioned, is a term used by Spinoza to mean not having a cause) and existing necessarily are important for Spinoza's pantheism because his entire theory is constructed on the basis of these two notions. All other propositions follow from either one of these two concepts. If substance's lack of need for a cause and its necessary existence is not proven then two consequences follow. If substance's lack of need for a cause is not proven for substance, then the proposition that it is not possible for more than one substance to exist in reality is no longer tenable, which means that multiple substances can be asserted. This is because Spinoza's assertion that there cannot be more than one substance depends on substance not having a cause for its existence. If necessary existence is not proven for substance or any other being, the existence of a being that exists necessarily and causes all other existing beings can be denied and hence a natural philosophy can be asserted without the existence of a Necessary Being. It makes no difference how substance is interpreted, whether it is interpreted as an unknown thing or as universal order of things, in any of these cases its necessary existence has been claimed and if the claim is fallacious then the pantheism falls apart.[69] For example, even if substance is taken as universal order of things, still if it does not exist necessarily then it simply means that the universal order of things is contingent and subject to change.

Spinoza's argument for the substance not having a cause is both invalid and uses unsound premises. Spinoza's entire proof for why substance is self-caused (i.e. its essence includes existence) is based on the idea that one substance cannot cause another. He argues that if one substance is to cause the existence of another then it is either the case that the second substance has identical attributes to the first substance or that it has different attributes. If it has identical attributes then there cannot be any distinction made between them and therefore there is only one substance. On the other hand if the two substances have different

---

[69] Henry E. Allison in his book titled *Benedictus de Spinoza: An Introduction* interprets substance as, "order of nature conceived as the source, or ground, of things and their intelligibility…". Henry E. Allison, *Benedictus de Spinoza: An Introduction* (New Haven: Yale University Press, 1987), 48.

attributes then it is impossible for one substance to cause the existence of another substance with different attributes, the reason being, as mentioned above in section one, an entity cannot give what it does not have (i.e. if it lacks the attribute itself it cannot cause something else to have that attribute).

However, the premises for such an argument are fallacious and its fallacy is due to a hidden premise which assumes only two alternatives. Spinoza seems to assert that when a substance causes another substance to exist then either the substance-effect has to be identical to substance-cause or they have to be completely different. However, this does not necessarily have to be the case. Gottfried Wilhelm Freiherr von Leibniz (1646-1716 A.D.) had objected to Spinoza's argument for why there cannot be more than one substance. According to Leibniz, it can be the case that two substances have some but not all attributes in common. For example if substance A has attributes x and y and substance B has attributes x and z, then the two substances can be distinguished from each other while they are both substances.[70] Even though what Leibniz points out still fails to undermine Spinoza's argument for why one substance cannot cause another substance to exist (because Substance A still cannot cause substance B since it does not have attribute z), nevertheless using similar lines of reasoning another argument could be constructed for why one substance can cause the existence of another.[71]

---

[70]Allison, "Benedictus de Spinoza: An Introduction," 52.

[71]Some might argue that Leibniz's argument still proves that there can be more than one substance. However, proving there can be more than one substance is not sufficient. Leibniz needs to also prove how an infinite substance can cause finite substances to exist. When there is a substance A with attributes x and y and a

For example it can be the case that substance A with attributes x, y, z causes to exist substance B with attribute z only. Hence, substance B is distinguished from substance A due to what it lacks, that is the attributes that it lacks (i.e. substance Axyz is different to substance Bz because substance A has more attributes than B).

In his book titled *Benedictus de Spinoza: An Introduction*, Henry E. Allison makes the point that Spinoza might have been trying to argue for the impossibility of the existence of more than one substance through the infinity of substance. Allison states that Spinoza seems to be aiming to prove that substance can only be infinite and hence if substance can only be infinite then it must have infinite attributes (which according to Spinoza, means that it has all attributes that there is to have). [72] If substance can only be infinite then it is impossible for one substance to create another because there cannot be two substances with infinite attributes. As a result the criticism above no longer applies.

---

substance B with attributes x and z, then the question arises as to how can substance A cause substance B to exist since substance A lacks attribute z. My own argument presented above subsequent to that of Leibniz, shows how an infinite substance can cause finite substances to exist while the latter is distinguished from the former (as in it is not one with the former). This argument too can face criticisms regarding the issue of comparison between infinite and finite beings (i.e., there is no comparison between infinite and finite substances), something which will not be discussed in this work. However, this is not an important issue that will affect the main discussion in this essay and subsequent arguments that will be presented for the impossibility of any union between the Necessary Being and a contingent being does not make use of this argument. The only intention of this argument is to demonstrate that Spinoza's argument fails.

[72]Allison, "Benedictus de Spinoza: An Introduction," 54.

However, if according to Allison's it was the case that Spinoza aimed to prove that there cannot exist more than one substance through his proof for the infinity of substance, then Spinoza begs the question. Spinoza's own argument for why substance is infinite (and indivisible) with infinite attributes, depends on the idea that there cannot be more than one substance (i.e., one substance cannot cause the existence of another, as discussed in detail in section one of this essay). On the other hand, his argument for why there cannot be more than one substance (or why one substance cannot cause the existence of another) depends on the idea that substance is infinite with infinite attributes (as Allison states) and hence, Spinoza begs the question.[73]

In fact the fallacy in Spinoza's arguments for the infinity of substance and its attributes does not stop at what was just illustrated. As it was already mentioned in section one, Spinoza claims that his evidence for why one substance can have more than one attribute depends on his proofs for oneness, infinity, indivisibility and eternity of substance.

---

[73]Spinoza's definition for an attribute as, "that which the intellect perceives as constituting the essence of a substance" (as mentioned in section 1) does not help the circularity of his argument. This definition does not mean that a person cannot perceive that which constitutes the essence of substance A and that which constitutes the essence of substance B and so on. In other words Spinoza has to prove that there is only one substance and therefore the mind can only perceive that which constitutes the essence of that one substance. In order to achieve the aforementioned aim Spinoza has to prove that each substance has infinite attributes (Spinoza, "Ethics," Part 1, Note for proposition X, 7.). However, before proving that substance has infinite attributes he has to prove that substance is infinite (Spinoza, "Ethics," Part 1, Proposition VIII, 4.). In order to prove that substance is infinite he relies on the premises that there cannot be more than one substance and that one substance cannot cause another (Spinoza, "Ethics," Part 1, Proof, Note I and Note II for proposition VIII and Proof for proposition VII, 4-5.). These last premises can only be accepted if each substance is assumed to have infinite attributes and hence the circularity.

However Spinoza's proof for the oneness, infinity, indivisibility and eternity of substance all assume that substance has more than one attribute (i.e., infinite attributes), which means that again Spinoza begs the question.

Setting aside Spinoza's proof for the infinity of substance and simply asserting that substance is infinite does not help his argument either. By stating that substance is infinite, it does not mean that other substances that are distinguished from the infinite substance cannot exist. As already hinted, it can be the case that there are substances with limited attributes which are distinguished from the infinite substance because of their finitude. For example, the infinite substance has attributes x1, x2, x3, x4 and so on to infinity, while a finite substance has for example only attribute x2, or attributes x2 and x3 and so on. It has to be pointed out that the distinction between infinite substance and finite substance is not a spatial one so that the existence of a finite substance would somehow limit the existence of the infinite substance. The distinction is solely based on the quantity of attributes and as such there is no contradiction in asserting the existence of a substance with infinite attributes, distinct from the existence of a substance or substances with finite attributes.

Hence, it seems that Spinoza's argument for substance not having a cause is either based on fallacious premises or that it is circular.

Spinoza does not do much better with the ontological arguments he presents for substance necessarily being existent. Spinoza's first ontological argument depends on the propositions that substance includes existence in its essence (i.e. what Spinoza labels self-caused) and because his argument for substance including existence in its essence has been refuted, then his first ontological argument fails as well. But say that, just for the sake of saving Spinoza's argument, it does not have to be proven that substance necessarily includes existence in its essence for Spinoza's argument to work and simply taking into consideration the notion of an entity that includes existence necessarily in its essence is sufficient for constructing such an argument.

Nevertheless the argument fails and its flaw is in the fact that Spinoza, failed to distinguish between the 'notion' of existence and its 'extension'.[74] When this distinction is made, many so called ontological arguments lose their tenability. To illustrate this point, consider the distinction between definitional predication of concepts and extensional predication of concepts.[75] Two concepts can be predicated to each other by definition even if they are not predicated to each other in an existing thing (that is even if they are not instantiated in the real world) and such a predication is definitional predication of concepts. For example, it could be said that, "A phoenix is blue". In reality there is no such creature as a phoenix, let alone a blue one, however, one can imagine a phoenix (i.e., one can have

---

[74]Extension is not used here in the same sense that Spinoza uses the term as one of the attributes of substance, the modification of which is corporeality. Extension is used here to refer to the object of a concept which exists in reality.

[75]The distinction presented between definitional and extensional predication of concepts is a distinction made by the author of the essay. This distinction is inspired by another type of distinction known as predication as essence and predication as extension made by Sadr al-Din al- Shirazi (1571-1640). However, it is only similar to that distinction in regards to one of its aspects, namely, distinction between mental operations and external reality. The distinction made by al-Shirazi takes into account other aspects as well such as the difference between essential and accidental properties.

the concept of the phoenix in his/her mind) and can predicate the colour blue (one can predicate the concept blue, as well as other colours, which is in his/her mind) to that phoenix (phoenixes, being fire birds, are actually described as being red or orange).

On the other hand, when two concepts are predicated to each other in reality, that is that both concepts are instantiated in an existing thing, then they are predicated to each other by extensional predication. For example in the case where it is said, "The statue of liberty is green", both the concept of 'statue of liberty' and the concept 'green' are predicated to each other in reality (notwithstanding the fact that the conception of colour is to a certain degree subjective). Hence, if an argument is to have validity its premises must have identical forms of predication and because the premises of Spinoza's argument do not have the same form of predication then his argument is invalid and hence does not prove its conclusion. In order to demonstrate the aforementioned invalidity, consider the syllogistic form of Spinoza's ontological argument:

Premise 1.   That which includes existence in its essence is the same as that which does not accept non-existence in its essence.

Premise 2.   That which does not accept non-existence in its essence is that which necessarily exists.

Premise 3.   Therefore that which includes existence in its essence is that which exists necessarily.

In the first premise the two terms, that is to say the term 'that which includes existence in its essence' and the term 'that which does not accept non-existence in its essence' are predicated to each other by definitional predication. Hence, since the notion of existence is necessarily contradictory to the notion of non-existence, then that notion which includes existence necessarily is equal to that notion which does not accept non-existence. On the other hand, the terms of the second premise, that is to say the terms 'that, which does not accept non-existence in its essence' and 'that which exists necessarily', are predicated to each other by extensional predication. This can be noticed from the fact that in the second premise an existent entity is asserted through the word 'that' and then necessary existence is predicated to it. In other words, it is stated that if there is an existent thing in reality that has an essence which does not accept non-existence then that entity necessarily exists. Hence, what appears to be the middle term of the two premises are in fact not the same thing and this can be demonstrated by reconstructing the argument to show their form of predication:

Premise 1.   The notion of that which includes existence in its essence is the same as the notion of that which does not accept non-existence in its essence.

Premise 2.   That (referring to an existing thing), which does not accept non-existence in its essence is that (referring to an existing thing again) which necessarily exists.

Premise 3.   Therefore the notion of that which includes existence in its essence is 'that' (referring to an existing entity) which exists necessarily.

When the argument is reconstructed showing its form of predication it becomes apparent that the term 'the notion of that which does not accept non-existence in its essence' is not the same as the term 'that (referring to an existing thing), which does not accept non-existence in its essence' and hence the middle terms are not identical. Only if the two notions of the first premise are proven to be instantiated in reality then the argument is valid, however on its own the argument is not valid. In order to prove the instantiation of the first premise, an argument has to be constructed which proves that an entity which includes existence in its essence exists in reality, a task which was suppose to be fulfilled by Spinoza's ontological argument.[76]

When the distinction between definitional and extensional predication is taken into consideration, Spinoza's ontological argument falls apart. A similar argument can be constructed against Spinoza's third ontological argument but it is not necessary as it does not serve the purpose of this book.

Spinoza's second ontological argument contains two independent arguments. One of these arguments is just the first ontological argument which has already been refuted. However, Spinoza puts forward another

---

[76]It might be argued that Spinoza has fulfilled this task in proposition VII where he supposedly proves that existence appertains to the nature of substance. However, that is an incorrect assumption. All that Spinoza has done is prove that if there was such a substance in reality then it would have existence included in its nature. The argument considered above is the argument that was supposed to prove that such a substance exists. Anyhow, even if it is given that the aim of proposition VII is to prove the existence of a substance which includes existence in its essence, it nevertheless is based on the notion that more than one substance cannot exist, a notion which Spinoza fails to prove (as indicated before). Hence, even in such a case Spinoza's ontological argument fails.

argument for the necessary existence of substance which depends on his definition of what it means to be non-existent. If something is non-existent then either its cause for its non-existence is from within itself or from other than itself. It cannot be from within itself because that would be admitting the existence of substance. It cannot be from other than itself because again that would be admitting to the existence of substance, since only that with the same nature as substance can cause its non-existence.

Spinoza's own definition of the cause of non-existence of things actually is more damaging for his arguments than beneficial. For one thing, if the cause of a thing's non-existence that is from other than itself has to be of exact same nature then a circle (or a circular object) cannot be the cause of the non-existence of a square-circle. Remember that Spinoza does not believe that it is the contradictory nature of square in comparison to circle that does not allow them to be united in an object but that it is the nature of circle that is the cause of the non-existence of a square-circle (or the nature of square that is the cause of the non-existence of the square-circle). Hence, the question has to be asked how it is that a circle that is not the same nature as a square-circle can be the cause for the non-existence of a square circle.

Similarly the assertion (since Spinoza's assertion that substance can only be conceived through itself is arbitrary) can be made that square-circle can only be conceived through itself and therefore if the existence of a square-circle is denied by claiming that the cause for its non-existence is from within, then the existence of a square-circle is admitted.[77]   Hence, square-circle must exist (has necessary existence)!

It seems that Spinoza has failed to prove the major principles which he needs to construct his pantheistic theory, namely, substance not needing a cause for its existence and existing necessarily (or as Spinoza terms it being self-caused) and the impossibility of more than one substance existing.[78]

One of the major components of Spinoza's philosophy is his identification of nature with God. In fact it could be argued that it was that God-nature unity which distinguishes Spinoza from other western philosophers of his time, not his arguments for self-causation and necessary existence of substance. The whole notion of pantheism in fact rests on the notion of God and nature being one. It was such a theory that moved western philosophy from an anthropomorphic way of looking at things and God to the more naturalistic definition of the world. As a bonus this pantheistic view was supposed to have managed to overcome many criticisms that were directed towards theistic arguments, for example the problem of God's creation existing independently to God

---

[77]The current work does not discuss Spinoza's assertion that an entity which is self-caused (i.e. exists necessarily) has to be conceived through itself because the assertion is simply without proof and arbitrary.   The least that could be claimed is that the notion of a necessarily existent entity is known through the concepts of existence and necessity, both, concepts which can apply to things other than substance.

[78]Spinoza bases his pantheism on the proposition that substance exists necessarily and cannot be caused by another substance hence replacing the notion of self-causality (as explained in this essay) with self-subsistence does not help Spinoza to prove his major principles.

after its original creation, or the problem of how God can be infinite if there are entities that exist separate to him.[79]   Nevertheless a philosophical theory has to be accepted based on its tenability. Until this point Spinoza has not presented any tenable arguments for constructing a sound pantheistic theory. The discussion of the following section will demonstrate that the flaw does not lie with Spinoza but pantheism in general.

Contradiction of pantheism

As it was mentioned before, the fallacy of Spinoza's pantheism is due to a contradiction that is also present in other versions of pantheism, namely that the Necessary Being is one with or is a contingent being.[80]   In this section, this issue will be addressed. First, the impossibility of any kind of union between the Necessary Being and contingent being/s will be demonstrated. Then, arguments will be put forward that entities which change are necessarily contingent beings. It will be argued that because material substance changes (or any other types of substances which changes), then it must be a contingently existing being. It will then be argued that, since material substance is a contingently existing being, it cannot be in union with or be a necessarily existing being.

---

[79]Stuart Hampshire, *Spinoza* (London: Faber and Faber), 32-33.

[80]Later the difference between my definition of contingent being and Spinoza's definition will be elucidated and it will be demonstrated that Spinoza's definition of *natura naturata* is actually what is in the philosophical sense termed a contingent entity.

It should be noted that it is possible that there are existent entities which exist but do not change. In the first part of this section it will be argued that whether or not a contingent being changes does not make any difference to the fact that it cannot be the Necessary Being. This is because the contradiction entailed in the union between necessary and contingent being/s is not dependent on change.

The Impossibility of Union between Necessary and Contingent Beings

The contradictory meaning of necessity and contingency is sufficient to point out that a being which exists necessarily cannot exist contingently. However, this point will be elaborated on for clarification. Before proceeding further, it is important to define two main terms that will be used in this discussion, namely the terms 'necessary existence' and 'contingent existence'. It is important to define these terms due to the strange definition that Spinoza gives the term 'contingent'. Ordinarily, the term contingent is used in the philosophical vocabulary to refer to an entity which existence is not necessary for it. In other words, the term contingent is used to refer to that entity, the essence of which does not include existence and which depends on another being for its existence. Spinoza, on the other hand, as it has already been mentioned in section one, argues that the term contingent can only be applied to those entities that are not predestined to exist in a particular way. That entity which is determined[81] to exist in a particular way, which its essence does not include existence and which depends on another entity for its existence (i.e., depends on the substance), Spinoza terms *natura naturata*[82], or as it is commonly translated 'nature passive' (by which Spinoza means modifications). However, it has to be pointed out that whether or not an entity is destined to exist in a particular way does not affect the ontological status of that entity.

Consider entity X. Entity X is a being which does not include existence in its essence, is dependent on another being for its existence (i.e., dependent on another being to cause its existence) and it is predestined to exist in a particular way. Now consider entity Y. Entity Y is a being that does not include existence in its essence and is dependent on another being for its existence (i.e., dependent on another being to cause its existence) but is not predestined to exit in a particular way. The question is whether or not, in terms of their ontological status, there is any difference between entity X and entity Y. It is immediately discovered that whether or not the two entities are predestined to exist in a particular way does not make any difference to the fact that both of them do not include existence in their essence and that they depend on another for their existence. Hence, it could be argued that Spinoza's distinction between contingent beings and beings which fall under the category of *natura naturata* is not an ontological distinction (even if Spinoza himself might claim it to be) but one relating to whether an entity is determined

---

[81]Spinoza, "Ethics," Part 1, Proposition XXXIII, 26.

[82]Spinoza, "Ethics," Part 1, Proof for proposition XXIX, 24. For Spinoza's explanation about modes depending on substance for their existence and continued existence see: Spinoza, "Ethics," Part 1, Proposition XXIV, 21.

for a particular action or not. This is because even if an entity is determined by the Necessary Being to exist or exist in a particular way (which this essay does not deny), still its existence being determined depends on the Necessary Being. In other words, without the Necessary Being it could not be determined to exist or exist in a particular way.[83]

Consequently, based on what was just discussed, the term contingent will not be used in the Spinozistic sense but will be used to refer to those entities which fall both under the category of *natura naturata* and what Spinoza calls contingent. Hence, the term contingent will be used to refer to that entity which does not include existence in its essence and which depends on another for its existence and continued existence.[84]

Spinoza uses the term 'necessary existence' in the same way that it is used in most philosophical vocabulary. A necessarily existing being is that being which exists independently of any other being and which therefore does not need another being for its existence. Once the two terms have been clarified the contradiction in pantheism can be demonstrated. To achieve this task the principle of causality needs to be considered first.

[83]Given that a plausible argument could be presented that would prove that all entities which are caused to exist by the Necessary Being must have been caused to exist in that way and no other way (i.e., it is impossible for them to have existed in any other way), still it does not mean that their existence is independent of the Necessary Being. In fact, it still means that their existence is dependent on the Necessary Being causing them.

[84]It cannot be asserted that my arguments for the impossibility of any kind of union between the Necessary Being and contingent being cannot undermine Spinoza's argument because Spinoza does not admit to the existence of any contingent being. This is because in my argument contingent being refers to an entity that depends on another entity for its existence and continued existence. This term can be applied both to those entities which Spinoza labels *natura naturata* and those entities for which he uses the term contingent.

Causality can be divided into several categories. Among these categories is what is known as the existential cause of an entity. The existential cause of an entity is different to other causes in the sense that it causes an entity's existence. Due to the fact that an entity's being is caused by its existential cause then its existence necessarily depends on that cause.

Quite often existential cause is confused with other types of causes. For example, when person A piles up books on top of each other to make a tower, that person imagines that he/she is the cause of the existence of that tower. But such a claim is far from the truth. First, the books existed before person A ever stacked them in a pile. Hence, the existence of the component parts of the tower does not depend on person A. Second, even when those books are stacked on top of each other, what keeps them in their position is not person A, it is the properties of its component parts (for example solidity) and the natural laws that apply to its environment (such as gravity, certain atmospheric pressure and so on). Consequently, person A cannot be said to be the existential cause of the tower of books but some other type of cause. An entity, however, is necessarily dependent on its existential cause for its existence because if it was not for that cause it could never exist. Hence, the very reality of an entity is in need of its existential cause and not only its form (such as in the case of the example of the tower). Because the very reality of a being is dependent on its existential cause for existence it can never become independent of that cause in terms of its existence, or else it would be the case that its reality can have existence by other than its existential cause (for example itself) and that would be contradictory to the fact that its reality has as its cause, its existential cause.

Spinoza does recognise the fact that the existence of an effect is dependent on its existential cause, however, he does not seem to notice the consequence of such a claim in regards to the union between something which has necessary existence and something which has contingent existence.

An entity which exists but is not dependent on any other for its existence exists necessarily. It is impossible for it not to exist because for something to stop existing, its existential cause has to stop sustaining its existence. However, the existence of that which exists independently of any other entity is not dependent on any other entity and therefore it does not have an existential cause to stop sustaining its existence.

On the other hand, an entity which exists but is dependent on another being for its existence is a contingent entity (which in the definition given to it in this work includes *natura naturata* and what Spinoza labels contingent). The other being which the contingent entity is dependent on has caused the existence of the contingent being and continues to sustain its existence. It is impossible for a contingent being to exist (or continue to exist) unless there is another beside it which gives it its existence and sustains that existence.[85]

A note should be added at this point about whether or not a being can begin to exist without a cause. Some, for example, have assumed that it is

---

[85]Spinoza, "Ethics," Part 1, Proposition XXIV, 21.

possible for a being to just occur spontaneously and by accident. However, in the same way that it was demonstrated above that the predestination of a contingent entity does not affect the fact that it needs a cause, it can be demonstrated that the spontaneous or accidental occurrence of an entity does not affect the ontological status of an entity either (i.e., an entity which begins to exist needs a cause for its existence whether it is predestined to exist or not). An entity which begins to exist does not include existence in its nature. If it included existence in its nature or essence then it would have existed. It is not impossible for it to exist either, since it begins to exist. Consequently, the said entity's nature can be said to need a cause to either exist or not existence.

The cause for the non-existence of an entity is the lack of an existential cause. On the other hand, the cause for the existence of an entity is its existential cause. The existential cause has to exist itself before it can give existence to another entity. If the claim is made that such an entity could exist without a cause then it has to be admitted that existing is part of its nature and necessary for it. However, it is contradictory to assert that an entity which it is possible for it to both exist and not exist includes existence in its nature necessarily. Hence, an entity which begins to exist whether spontaneously or by accident still needs a cause for its existence.[86]

---

[86]There is actually no need for this argument because causality, despite being rejected by some (such as David Hume (1711-1776) and humean philosophers), is an inescapable reality. To admit to entities beginning to exist without any cause is not only contrary to reason, but also such a belief renders any philosophical and scientific discussion untenable. Philosophical discussions and in fact any form of reasoning is dependent on an argument's premises causing its conclusion. If it is possible for things to occur without any cause then there is no reason to believe that the conclusion which is achieved through philosophical reasoning follows from its premises rather than just something which has occurred without any

It should, however, be mentioned that it is not being asserted that there can be any accidental events. One agrees with (to a degree) Spinoza that entities that are caused to exist by the Necessary Being are predestined to exist as they do. However, the demonstration above was only to show that even if it is not accepted that things are predestined still because they are contingent (in the sense that they do not exist necessarily and are dependent on another being for their existence), they need a cause.

By now the course of the argument might have become apparent. If the Necessary Being is also a contingent being then it is both independent in regards to its existence and dependent in regards to its existence. It is both the case that it does not need any other entity for its existence and that it needs another entity for its existence. It cannot be claimed that the other entity which the contingent entity needs for its existence is itself, because that would be saying that the contingent entity does not need any other entity for its existence (i.e., it is independent in regards to its existence) and that is contradictory to the claim that it needs another entity for its existence.

With this simple demonstration the impossibility of any kind of union between a necessarily existing entity and a contingent entity is demonstrated. This demonstration can be summarized in the following way:

> 1. If X is a necessarily existing being then *it is not dependent on any other for its existence*, which means **it can exist by itself**

reason. In this sense there is no way to argue for any conclusion and only severe skepticism has to be admitted (even that cannot be admitted since there is no reason to believe it).

2. If X is a contingent being then *it is dependent on another for its existence*, which means **it cannot exist by itself**.

3. Therefore, if X is both a necessarily existing being and a contingent being then X **can both exist and not exist by itself** (*or it is both dependent and not dependent on another for its existence*).

4. Due to contradiction contained in 3, X cannot be both a necessarily existing being and a contingent being.

5. Therefore X has to be **either** a necessarily existing entity or a contingent entity.

As it can be noticed, the demonstration presented above does not require that a contingent being should change, the mere fact that the contingent being is contingent means it cannot be a necessary being.

A necessarily existing being is said to include existence in its nature or essence. The reason for this is that since a necessarily existing entity does not receive its existence from any other entity it must therefore include its existence within itself. On the other hand, a contingent entity (according to the definition presented above and not that of Spinoza's) is said to not include existence in itself because it needs another being in order to exist. Spinoza also categorizes entities into that entity which includes existence in its essence (i.e., substance) and those entities which do not include existence in their essence (i.e., modifications).[87] Hence, without considering any other argument besides the one that has already been presented, there is sufficient proof to show the untenability of

---

[87] Spinoza, "Ethics," Part 1, Proposition XX, 19; Spinoza, "Ethics," Part 1, Proposition XXIV, 21.

Spinoza's pantheism. Spinoza's argument is untenable because it asserts that a necessarily existing entity is also a contingent entity.[88] In other words, Spinoza's pantheism states that an entity which includes existence in its essence does not include existence in its essence.

The aforementioned argument demonstrated the impossibility of any union between a being which existence is necessary for it and a contingent being. However, its demonstration is based solely on Spinoza's premises. On the other hand, there is no reason to think that others cannot improve on Spinoza's argument. For example, it might be admitted that it is in fact impossible to have any kind of union between a necessarily existing entity and a contingently existing entity but it was never the case that such a union was being admitted in the first place. It can be claimed that what is ordinarily viewed as a contingent entity, such as the different entities in the material world, are actually necessarily existing beings (for example the whole of the universe or material universe is a necessarily existing being). There are several different ways to approach such a criticism, however only one will be considered in this essay, namely the argument from change.[89]

---

[88]To demonstrate that the predestination of an entity does not affect the argument presented in the text, the following argument can be put forward. An entity is either predestined to exist by another entity or is not predestined to exist by another entity (i.e., it exists because of itself). If it is predestined to exist by another entity then it cannot not be predestined to exist by another entity, since that is a contradiction in terms. Hence, it is logically impossible for an entity which is predestined to exist by another entity (i.e., modes) to not be predestined by another (i.e., the Necessary Being); or in other words a contingent being (i.e., a being which is predestined) cannot be one with a Necessary Being (i.e., a being which is not predestined).

[89]Other arguments can also be put forward, such as the argument that divisible entities cannot have necessary existence. The argument proceeds something like

In the next part it will be argued that things that change cannot have necessary existence. Consequently, since matter changes (or any other substance that changes), then it cannot be an entity which existence is necessary for it. As it was already noted before, the argument from change does not prove the impossibility of union between a necessarily existing entity and a contingent entity, that conclusion was demonstrated above. The argument from change only indicates that entities which change are contingent beings. To prove changing entities are not necessary beings the argument that was presented above has to be added to the argument from change.

Contingency and Change

For something (for example, substance) to change no matter whether only a small part of it changes or all of it changes, the mere fact of change indicates an entity which does not exist necessarily. It makes no difference whether change is claimed in regards to the accidents of a substance or to the whole of the entity. Take the example of a red box, redness being the accident of the substance which is the box. Hence, if this red box changes to a green box even though the underlying substratum remains the same, its accident changes. But for a red box to

---

the following: Entities that are divisible are in need of their parts in order to exist. Because such entities are in need of their parts in order to exist then it means that they are dependent on their parts for their existence. There is not sufficient space in this footnote to discuss the detail of this argument; it was only mentioned for referential reasons.

become green it needs to acquire the property of greenness or the property which causes greenness, because greenness is not in the essence of the red box (or the property which causes greenness is not in the essence of the red box). Now assuming that the red box is a necessarily existent thing (withstanding the arguments given for the impossibility of a corporeal and/or limited object existing necessarily) then that which produces the property of greenness, not existing in the necessarily existing thing, exists contingently. But for the box to be green it needs to include greenness in it that is to say, it needs to be united with that which produces the property of greenness. Hence, to state that the red box is a necessarily existing object which has acquired the property of greenness which is a contingently existing property is the same as stating that a necessarily existing object has become a contingent object and that is a contradiction in terms.

It has to be pointed out that the aforementioned argument depends on the impossibility of more than one object for which existence is necessary for it. Hence, for the argument to be tenable, it has to be proven that it cannot be the case that more than one object for which existence is necessary can exist (i.e. it cannot be the case that both the red box and that which produces the property of greenness exist necessarily). Spinoza's argument for a substance that includes change within it is also based on impossibility of more than one necessarily existing entity (this will be discussed below).

As for the argument for the impossibility of the existence of more than one necessarily existing object, again such an argument relies on the fact that a necessarily existing object cannot be united with an object that exists contingently. If there were more than one necessarily existing object then there has to be an aspect which distinguishes one necessarily existing object from the other (as Spinoza also points out). That aspect or property which distinguishes between the two necessarily existing objects cannot be contingent because it can be the case that something can have necessary existence without having that property. For example, assume that A and A2 are both necessary beings for which existence is a necessity (it is impossible for them not to exist and they both do not have a cause for their existence). For A to be distinguished from A2 there needs to be a distinguishing property, say the attribute of 2, but it can be the case that A can be necessary without the attribute of 2 (that is the necessity of A is not from the attribute of 2 but from being A) and hence it is not necessary for 2 to exist which means 2 is contingent. Hence, A2 is a being which has both necessary and contingent existence.

However, an assertion can be made that 2 is also a necessary being which causes the distinction between the two necessary beings. But that would be claiming that there are three necessary beings and hence these three again need to be distinguished from each other and again they have to be either distinguished from each other through contingent beings or more necessary beings. In the former case, it is impossible due to the fact that necessary existence cannot be united with contingent existence and in the latter case the necessary beings will never be distinguished because their distinction depends on an infinite regress.

Let us assume the change is not an accidental change but change to the whole of the entity, say for example when ice turns into water. In such a case, either it is claimed that the underlying substratum remains the same (for example, iceness remains the same) and only its 'accidents' change (for example, the accident of liquidity is acquired while the accident of solidity is lost) or that the substratum also changes. In the former case the same argument that was put forward above for why a necessarily existing entity cannot be united with an entity which has contingent existence (that is the accident that has been acquired) also applies in this case. If it is claimed that the substratum changes then because it acquired a property in its being which it did not have before then it could not have been the cause of it itself (or according to Spinoza one attribute cannot be the cause of another). Because the entity that has changed substantially is not the cause of its own change then it must be the case that something other than it has caused that change, which means either there are two necessarily existing beings or that which has changed is contingent. For example, in the ice-water instance, it could be stated that since ice does not have the property of liquidity it needs an external cause to give it that property and the rest of the argument then follows.[90]

Spinoza accepts that a necessary being cannot change.[91] Furthermore, Spinoza seems to accept that change requires an external cause. These

---

[90]It could be claimed that what ice lacks within itself is heat (or sufficient amount of heat), that is the property of heat and hence it lacks the property of liquidness due to lack of heat (or attribute of heat) and when it has heat then its substratum acquires the property of liquidity.

[91]Spinoza, "Ethics," Part 1, Proof for proposition XXXIII, 26-29. Spinoza states: "Now if they say this, they must also admit that God can change his decree. For had God decreed otherwise than he has concerning nature and her order, that

two points, he does not dispute. What he does disagree with is that the corporeal world is a changing entity. Spinoza uses Schuller's theory of motion in defence of his assertion.[92] Spinoza asserts that even though there might be motion and change within an entity because the proportion of motion in comparison with rest remains the same in that entity then that entity can be considered as one unchanging entity.

> ...an individual whose parts, i.e. all bodies, vary in infinite
> ways, without any change of the whole individual.

Spinoza's argument for the immutability of the world depends on two premises. First, that change is affirmed after motion and second, that difference in proportionality equals change (i.e. something only changes if it has changed in regards to proportionality). Spinoza's first premise cannot be denied, that is change is certainly affirmed after motion, but it is not only motion that affirms change. On the other hand, Spinoza's second premise has to be viewed in a more critical manner. It can be agreed with Spinoza that change can be linked to some sort of proportionality. In other words when a being changes either it loses a property or gains a property. But how this proportionality is viewed is important. For example, consider figure 1.

---

is, had he willed and conceived anything else concerning nature, he must necessarily have some other intellect and will than those which he now has. And if it is permitted to attribute to God another will than those which he now has, without change in his essence or perfection, what would there be to prevent him from changing his decree concerning things created, and yet remain perfect. For his intellect and will concerning things created and their order is the same in respect to his essence and perfection...all the philosophers, I have seen, concede that no such thing as potential intellect in God can be granted, but only actual."

[92]Allison, "Benedictus de Spinoza: An Introduction," 72.

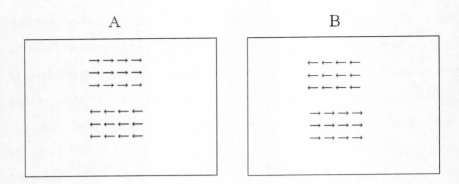

Figure 1

In the above figure, A has changed to B, its proportionality has remained the same in terms of the number of arrows it contains yet there is a difference between A and B and hence it has changed even though its proportion of arrows has remained the same. Thus, it is not the lack of difference in any kind of proportionality of its internal parts that indicates mutability. Even if the proportionality of motion and rest are the same in an entity nevertheless the different forms or attributes that the entity acquires as indicated by motion and rest (for example, the different form that the objects A acquired and hence became object B due to the difference in the position of the equally numbered arrows) proves change.

The arguments just presented surrounded the issue of whether or not a being that goes through change can be a necessarily existing being. It was demonstrated that it is impossible for the Necessary Being to change and hence, a being that changes is necessarily contingent.

An issue needs to be considered with regards to the idea that it is impossible for a being that exists necessarily to change. That issue is that the Necessary Being causes things to exist but is supposedly unchanging itself. The act of causing something to exist seems to indicate a change in the Necessary Being. If things did not exist until the Necessary Being caused them to exist then there must have been some kind of change in the Necessary Being. This problem cannot be dealt with comprehensively in this work; however some points can be stated which justify the conclusion which is being argued for (that conclusion being that a being which existence is necessary for it cannot change).

The aim of this part of the chapter was to demonstrate that it is impossible for a necessarily existing being to change. If such a conclusion has been reached, then even if such a conclusion creates mysteries in regards to how the necessarily existing being can cause the existence of contingent beings without changing, still it is in no way a reason to reject the conclusion as fallacious. There might be further arguments needed to demonstrate how the necessarily existing being can cause the existence of contingent beings without changing, however, the need for further arguments to prove such an issue does not affect the conclusion of the arguments given above.

Furthermore, it can be argued that the Necessary Being causes the existence of contingent beings without changing. The discussion above regarding the impossibility of any change in the Necessary Being demonstrates that anything which changes in regards to either its accident or its being cannot be a necessarily existing being. However, the

Necessary Being causing the existence of contingent beings does not in any way indicate change in the being of the Necessary Being.

Two Other Concerns

There are two more issues left to deal with in order to fully demonstrate the untenability of Spinoza's argument, both of which are raised by Stuart Hampshire, in his book *Spinoza*, namely the problem of the infiniteness of God and the difference between a transient and an immanent cause.

Hampshire while discussing the metaphysical theory of Spinoza gives the following argument for why God cannot be distinguished from nature (or his creation):

> If God is distinguished from nature, which he creates, then God cannot be infinite and all powerful, because there exists something other than, or distinguishable from, God, which limits God's power and perfection; on this assumption God cannot be either infinite or perfect, because ex hypothesi Nature, being distinguished from God, must posses some attributes which God does not posses.[93]

Hampshire takes the aforementioned argument from proposition four of part one of *Ethics* which as mentioned above states that things are distinguished from each other either by the difference of their attribute/s or the difference of their modifications (or effects). Hence, if two things are distinguished from each other by their attributes, it must be the case

---

[93]Hampshire, "Spinoza," 33.

that God is different from His creation because His creation has attributes which God does not. A God who lacks attributes which exist in other things is a finite God. It can be added to what Hampshire has stated that also if the effects of God has attributes that God does not have then the question has to be asked how did God create those entities, that is to say how could God create something which has attributes that he himself does not have. The latter assertion is actually another one of Spinoza's propositions in his discussion about substances not being able to create other substances with different attributes.

The problem just presented is not a new issue considered only by Spinoza and in fact the issue of how can God make a corporeal entity if it is not corporeal itself, goes back to early philosophical discussions. Aristotle's solution was that there is a corporeal entity separate to God that exists necessarily and that God simply acts on that corporeal entity. But such a solution is no solution at all because as it was demonstrated before that there cannot exist more than one necessarily existing entity. But all hope is not lost for those who assert the complete separation between the necessarily existent being and a contingent being. After all it was proven that a necessary existent being cannot be one with a contingent being so why should one contradiction be preferred over another (i.e. why should the union between the Necessary Being and contingent being be preferred over the idea that there are two necessary beings or that God has created a being with attributes it does not have, etc).

It is apparent from what was quoted above from Hampshire that Spinoza (as well as Hampshire) assumed any attribute to be a positive attribute and did not distinguish between positive and negative attributes. What that means is that when beings are considered, quite often concepts are attributed to them when in fact those concepts do not represent attributes that exist in an entity at all and in fact only represent lack of attributes. Take as an example the analogy of a dark room. The concept of darkness is quite often attributed to a room with no light when in reality darkness is not an attribute, that is to say not an existent attribute and it is simply a concept representing lack of an existent attribute that is the attribute of having light. Those concepts that represent lack of attributes are referred to as negative attributes. Hence, the word 'negative' is a representative of the notion 'lack of' which in turn is a representative of limitation. It could also be said that positive attributes indicate completeness or perfection in existence while negative attributes indicate limitations.

Taking the distinction between negative and positive attributes into account an argument could be put forward as follows. An entity which lacks necessary existence and depends on another existent entity to exist is limited and hence, has certain negative attributes. Those negative attributes is what distinguishes it from the necessary existence. Since negative attributes do not indicate completeness or perfection in existence and indicate limitation, then a being which has negative attributes does not in any way limit a being which has all the positive attributes infinitely and without limitations. Those attributes which indicate contingent existence are negative attributes and since extension and corporeality indicate contingent existence then they are negative attributes. Hence, extended corporeal things being separate to that which exists necessarily does not in any way limit the infinity or unlimited nature of that which exists necessarily.[94]

Another one of the issues which Hampshire points out in regards to Spinoza's arguments against a God which is separate to his creation is the issue of a transient versus immanent cause. Hampshire argues that if God is accepted as a transient cause rather than an immanent cause of the universe then God can only be accounted for when the creation of the universe is acknowledged but not the changes that occurs after that creation. If it is truly believed that God is the continuing cause of the universe then God has to be accepted as an immanent cause.[95]

It will be demonstrated that the Necessary Being cannot be the cause of change within itself, but even if such an argument is set aside still the separation of the Necessary Being from contingent beings does not necessarily equate that the latter has independent existence. In other words the proposition that contingent beings are separate in terms of their existence to the Necessary Being does not equate to the contingent beings not having dependence on the Necessary Being for their existence. The arguments for the impossibility of two necessary beings existing and Spinoza's assertion that the essence of a contingent being can never

---

[94]For example, through arguments that argue an entity the essence of which can be conceived does not exist necessarily, that which is comprised of parts does not exist necessarily or that which changes cannot exist necessarily, etc.

[95]Hampshire, "Spinoza," 34.

include existence, is sufficient for proving the continued dependence of the contingent beings on that which exists necessarily.

A necessarily existing being cannot be a cause of change within itself. Consider an entity, say entity A. If entity A is made up of parts then entity A is in need of those parts to exist and hence its existence is dependent on the existence of its parts. Hence, if entity A is made of parts then it cannot be a necessarily existing being. Spinoza accepts that a necessarily existing object cannot be divided into parts.[96]   Therefore, when a necessarily existing entity changes, then it changes in its entire reality and not just its parts.

Now, assume that entity A is a necessarily existing being which causes a change within itself. Since entity A is indivisible, then, when it changes it changes in its entirety and not only in regards to a part of itself. The changed entity can be labelled entity B. Entity B is an effect of entity A since entity B did not exist until entity A caused it to exist by causing a change within itself. Taking into consideration that an effect always needs its cause for continued existence (as argued for in this chapter), then, it has to be the case that entity B needs entity A for its continued existence because entity B is an effect of entity A. However, entity A no longer exists because now it is entity B, but that would mean that entity B no longer exists because its existential cause is no longer existent. It seems that the result of what has just been demonstrated is that entity A would terminate itself if it causes a change within itself. However, this is not the case because entity A cannot cause a change within itself in the

---

[96]Spinoza, "Ethics," Part 1, Proposition XII, 10.

first place. The change within entity A requires its cause for continued existence and because as soon as that change occurs then simultaneously the cause no longer exists, then the change does not occur in the first place. For the aforementioned reason, if it is accepted that the Necessary Being is indivisible and it is also accepted that an effect continuously needs its cause for its existence, then, it has to be accepted that a necessary being cannot cause change (or modification as Spinoza terms it) within itself.

In Europe, pantheism was purportedly developed by Spinoza and other philosophers in order to resolve some of the contradictions that the theistic accounts of God seem to contain. Coupled with the desire to resolve the problems of theistic interpretation of God was the atmosphere and culture in which pantheistic arguments were being developed. Empirical and experimental sciences had made great advancements in discovering many of the mysteries of nature and it was more and more the case that un-scientific claims of the church about the physical world were being refuted.[97] Hence, slowly the naturalistic way of looking at the world was replacing the anthropomorphic way that was dominant in the religions of that part of the world. But this trend had limited itself to the philosophical and theological discussions of only a limited part of the world. The theistic arguments available to Spinoza were mostly Catholic oriented and therefore anthropomorphic.[98] Hence,

---

[97]For example that the earth revolves around the sun.

[98]From the first verses of the old testament which states that God rested on the seventh day, to the verses that follow, which describes God as an 'angry' and 'temperamental' entity making mistakes, God is illustrated as having human attributes or what can more accurately be termed negative attributes. The doctrine

the pantheistic view seemed to be a view which gained momentum very quickly in Europe. However, the tenability of the pantheistic view does not depend on its socio-historical background. The arguments presented above demonstrated that not only it is the case that Spinoza's pantheism is untenable but also that pantheism in general seems to be untenable if it attempts to argues for its conclusion along similar line of reasoning as Spinoza did. The contradiction in pantheism is due to its assertion that a being for which existence is necessary (a Necessary Being) can be one with a contingent being (in the sense defined by the author of this essay). Since necessity is contradictory to contingency then it follows that pantheistic assertions are contradictory and therefore untenable. In addition, it does not make any difference whether necessary existence is called active nature and contingent existence as passive nature. If the two are one entity then it means that there exists an entity which is both active and passive and again that is a contradiction in terms.

Addendum

Spinoza's argument for the necessity in the action (which he sees as equivalent to lack of freewill) of the Necessary Being has not been elaborated on in this dissertation. Even though many pantheistic theorists purport the idea that the Necessary Being not having freewill

---

of trinity contained within the Catholic ideology and rigorously defended by many Catholic philosophers (such as Thomas Aquinas) views God anthropomorphically as at least being part man. Hence, this doctrine which dominated European theological and philosophical thought during Spinoza's time was subject to attack by Spinoza and many of his contemporaries.

versus it having freewill is the difference between pantheism versus theism, in reality freewill for the Necessary Being is not an aspect that can only be applied in a theistic theory of the world just as no lack of freewill in action is not an aspect that can only be applied to a pantheistic view of the world. There can be a theistic theory that claims distinction between God and nature yet still claim the lack of free will in God (that is to say that God is separate to His creation but does not create his creation with freewill). In the same way there can be a pantheistic theory that claims the unity of God and nature but accept into that theory the freewill of God that is united with nature. In other words, lack of freewill in regards to the necessary existence's action (if it can be called as such) is independent of the argument for whether or not the Necessary Being is one with nature.

There is, however, a small point that should be mentioned (though it will not be elaborated on in detail in the current work). Many philosophers, including Spinoza, have defined freewill as an entity's ability to change its decision. Consequently, because a Necessary Being cannot change, then the assertion cannot be made that it has freewill.[99] There is, however, another way to define freewill. An entity can be said to have freewill if it does not have anything other than itself limiting its action. An entity does not have freewill when there are things other than it that limit its action. In this sense, an entity that has necessary existence also has freewill, because it is not limited by anything. Therefore, it could be asserted that the Necessary Being (or God) has freewill because there is nothing other than itself that can limit it from causing things to exist. Since the

[99]Spinoza, "Ethics," Part 1, Proposition XXXIII, 26-29.

Necessary Being is the existential cause of contingent beings, therefore, it is necessarily the case that only it would cause things to exist as they do. This necessity is not a restriction that is caused by entities besides the Necessary Being itself. This means that it is the Necessary Being who wills things to happen as they do but it wills it as such by the necessity of its own self.

On the other hand, entities that do not have necessary existence, such as matter for example, are limited by things other than themselves which cause them to exist and act in a particular way (the existence of their action is also caused by the Necessary Being). Such entities do not have a will because they do not act according to themselves. Other entities, such as human beings for example, have limited freewill despite not having necessary existence. Human beings have freewill because they can act according to themselves. Their freewill is limited in the sense that such type of freewill has been caused to exist by the Necessary Being.

Because some philosophers have not distinguished between freewill and the lack of freewill in the aforementioned sense, they have defined the will of the Necessary Being in a mechanical way similar to that of matter described above. In either case, this discussion needs to be further elucidated for a comprehensive understanding of its various component parts which can be left for another work.

Reconciling Contradictions

There have been a few interpreters of Spinoza that have recognised that Spinoza's pantheism, or in fact any kind of pantheism, will eventually lead to the position that the Necessary Being is united with a contingent being and such a position makes a contradictory claim.   Hence, instead of attempting to find ways of eliminating this contradiction, they have decided to accept it and integrate it into their interpretation of Spinoza's pantheism.   However, it is a difficult task to mention all such attempts, which could even be a separate research topic on its own, but one interpretation stands out in the sense that answering the claims made in it could also serve as a reply to other similar interpretations.

William T. Stace in his book titled *Mysticism and Philosophy* takes up the discussion of Spinoza's pantheism by using mystical experience to evaluate the validity of pantheism in relation to theism.[100]   Stace concludes that pantheism in general and Spinoza's pantheism in particular is not a rational theory nor is it meant to be. The pantheistic view of the world is actually the mind's acknowledgement of the fact that the world exists in a contradictory state.[101] The world existing in a contradictory state does not mean, according to Stace, that a rational theory has to be developed that takes as its primary concept the acknowledgement of contradiction in every statement, for example as Hegel did, but to simply accept via empirical experience that the world exists in a contradictory state.[102]   According to Stace, God is both identical and distinct from

---

[100] W.T. Stace. *Mysticism and Philosophy.* New York: Jeremy P. Tarcher, 1960.

[101]Stace, "Mysticism and Philosophy," 217.

[102]Stace, "Mysticism and Philosophy," 241.

nature, he is both personal and impersonal and he is both evil and good![103]
Hence, pantheism is simply acknowledging this reality.

Stace begins by rejecting both the dualistic and monistic interpretations
of different mystics about their experience of the unity of the self with the
one (i.e. unity of the self with God).[104] He then concludes that because
none of the two contradictory interpretations apply, one has no choice
but to conclude that the only alternative interpretation of the unity of the
self with God is to accept that both sides of the contradictories apply.
Hence, it is both the case that the self is united with God and it is not. He
then applies this conclusion to the unity between God and nature and
states that in the same way God is both nature and not nature and uses
the notion of infinity and the concept of the problem of evil as
philosophical evidence for the support of his claim.

It has to be stated that the first argument, that is to say, that because
neither the dualistic interpretation nor the monistic interpretation apply
to mystical interpretations and hence both have to be accepted,
disregards logical principles in addition to epistemological principles in
order to reach an arbitrary conclusion. Firstly, both the dualistic and the
monistic interpretations given to mystical experience are to do with the
mystic's experience. Hence, it is perfectly valid to state that the mystic's

---

[103]Stace, "Mysticism and Philosophy," 246-247.

[104] Dualistic interpretation of mystical experiences of uniting with God
according to Stace is those that assert that despite the unification of the self with
God, the self remains distinct from God. Monistic interpretation of mystical
experiences of uniting with god according to Stace is those that assert that the self
becomes one with God. Stace, "Mysticism and Philosophy," 243-246.

experience does not prove anything in reality and is limited to the mystic's mind. If I dream about a hundred headed cow, despite the fact that such a dream might require deep psychological analysis of why I would have such a strange dream, it nevertheless does not prove that outside my mind in reality there exists hundred headed cows. Hence, the denial of both the dualistic and the monistic interpretation of the experience of a mystic is simply denial of contraries and not negation of contradictories. Hence both can be false, which would mean that neither the self of the mystic is united with God in a way that both God and the self remain distinct nor is the self united with God in a way that God and the self become one.   Both interpretations could be denied and it could be asserted that the self can never become united with God.

Stace's definition of infinity is no different to that of Hampshire's and hence that which was written above in reply to Hampshire's definition of infinity also applies to Stace's definition.[105]

It is important to point out that Stace's interpretation of Spinoza's philosophy is against the aim of Spinoza in *Ethics*. The purpose of *Ethics* was to provide a theory which was rational in the sense that the alternative to that philosophy was irrational and untenable. Spinoza did not aim to conclude in his *Ethics* that the world is an irrational place where conjunction of contradictories could exist (a proposition which Stace mistakenly associates to Spinoza).

---

[105]Stace, "Mysticism and Philosophy," 241-243.

3   UNITY OF EXISTENCE

There is a pantheistic theory that has been developed for almost four centuries by a number of Islamic philosophers and Gnostics, which, although quite different to Spinozistic pantheism in its discussion, it nevertheless has similarity with Spinoza's philosophy in terms of its conclusion.

The issue for Muslim philosophers was not to replace an anthropomorphic God with a natural one because the notion of an anthropomorphic God was never present in Islamic philosophy in the first place, especially those philosophies developed by Shia Muslim philosophers. These philosophers were more concerned with issues such as God's knowledge of his creation, how God creates or brings creation into existence (especially the issue of bringing into existence multitude of effects) and the notion of existence. [106] The first radical leap to address at

_____

[106] In Islamic philosophy knowledge is not seen as an anthropomorphic attribute but rather an attribute of existence. Hence, perfection in terms of knowledge is seen as an existential perfection. This is due to the fact that in Islamic philosophy, attributes are not categorized based on being anthropomorphic or non-anthropomorphic, rather attributes are categorized by the degree of existential perfection they represent. For example, knowledge represents an existential perfection (the degrees of which determine its degree of perfection) while ignorance represents a lack of existential attribute of knowledge. Hence, a being that has consciousness is said to be existentially more perfect than one that does not have consciousness, because the being with consciousness can have and acquire knowledge (note that in Islamic philosophy one that is conscious

least the first of these issues was taken by Shehaab al-Din Sohrawardi[107]

---

necessarily has knowledge of him/herself, of the notion of existence, the notion of reality and the notion of knowledge). The degree of knowledge also decides on the degree of existential perfection. It should be pointed out that what has just been said does not mean that human beings are regarded as having knowledge similar to God or that God has consciousness similar to human beings. All that is being asserted is that the attributes of knowledge or knowing is an existential perfection, although the act and nature of knowing itself can be or is different depending on the type of being.

Knowledge should not be labelled as being an anthropomorphic attribute limited to human beings alone, solely on the premises that human beings have knowledge. Based on such premises all attributes of human beings would be anthropomorphic. The reason why many philosophers might have mistaken knowledge as an anthropomorphic attribute, might have been due to the fact that the knowledge of other attributes of human beings, such as for example corporeality, are acquired through the senses while knowledge of knowledge is a concept not acquired through the senses (and even proven to be innate). Hence, the difference between attributes of entities that are known through the senses and those that are known innately could have led to the latter being labelled an anthropomorphic attribute.

The issue that is mentioned here is the question raised by some philosophers as to how it is that a multitude of effects could come about from a being that is indivisible. Some Muslim philosophers, among whom, was Ibn Sina (d. 1037), proposed intermediary intellects between the Necessary Being and His multitude of creation. It was proposed that these intellects are fully dependent on their preceding causes and which lead back to the Necessary Being. Further more, the multitude of creation that come from these intellects are also fully dependent on them which means they are also dependent on the Necessary Being. Therefore, according to the proponents of this theory there is only one act of creation from the Necessary Being which results in multitude of effects all of which are dependent on the Necessary Being. In later centuries other theories were developed by Shia Muslim philosophers and theologians to answer the problem of multitude of effects coming from the indivisible Being without proposing any intermediaries between the Necessary Being and His creation. The outcome resulted in the proposition that all creation is only one effect coming from the Necessary Being. However, the discussion of this subject requires much more space than is available in this footnote.

[107]Shehaab al-Din Abu al-Futuh Yahyaa ibn Habash ibn Amirak al-Sohrawardi also known as Shaikh al-Ishraaq (*Ishraaq* meaning illumination) lived between 1155 and 1191 and is most famous for his philosophy of illumination (*Hekmat-e-Eshraaq*). A critic of the way logical and metaphysical principles were presented by peripatetic Muslim philosophers before him, Sohrawardi presented his logical and metaphysical principles using the notion of lights. He is most famous for his

when he presented his theory of presence-knowledge.[108]   However, the theory that became both the most controversial and the most influential in terms of entering the notion of pantheism in the Islamic philosophical discussions was that of Sadr Al-Din Mohammad Shirazi, also known as Mollaa Sadraa, Sadr Mote'allehin and Aakhund.[109]

Sadr Din Shirazi based his entire metaphysical, epistemological and logical theory on his ontological findings, that is to say his study of existence.[110]   In Sadr Din Shirazi's philosophy, existence has primacy, that is to say that what is real is existence and all other things that are considered in philosophical discussions, such as for example quiddities[111]

---

theories regarding intuitive knowledge also known as *al-Ilm al-Hodhuri*. See: Suhrawardi. *The Philosophy of Illumination*, trans. John Walbridge & Hossein Ziai. Utah: Brigham University Press, 1999.

[108]Al-Ilm al-Hodhuri which is often translated as "knowledge by presence" was first proposed by Shehaab Al-Din Sohrawardi and later developed by subsequent Muslim philosophers belonging to the Shia theological school of thought (such as Sadr al-Din Shiraazi). The theory of presence-knowledge concentrates on the fact that the knower and its knowledge are one. Using his theory of knowledge by presence, Sohrawardi also attempted to solve the problem raised by some philosophers about the issue of the knowledge of God about his particular creations. See: Mehdi Ha'iri Yazdi. *The Principles of Epistemology in Islamic Philosophy: Knowledge by Presence.* New York: State University of New York Press, 1992.

[109]*Sadr* means "high" or in this case "foremost". *Mote'alleheen* is plural term meaning "teachers", hence *Sadr Mote'alleheen* means "the foremost among the teachers" and it was a title given to Sadr Al-Din Shirazi (1571-1640) for developing his philosophy of existence. Sadr Din Shirazi based his entire philosophy on the reality and meaning of existence.

[110]Sadr al-Din Shirazi in his most famous work, known as *Al-Hikmat Al-Muta'aliyah Fil-asfaar Al-'Aqliyah Al-Arba'ah or Asfaar* (Journeys) for short, delves into the study of being and existence. He concludes that existence is univocal in regards to every 'existent' thing and that it has principality over quiddity (*maahiya*) in contrast to being a mere predicate of essences.

[111]*Maahiyyat* translated here as "quiddity" can approximately be defined as a

or concepts in the field of epistemology, contingency and necessity in the field of modal logic and change in the field of metaphysics, are merely the mind's abstraction from the limitations and perfections of existence. For Sadr Din Shirazi the study of existence precedes all other studies because it is only through existence that notions and concepts are known. Therefore all things have to be considered in relation to existence and what is to be considered is their existence.

Sadr Din Shirazi comes to the conclusion of primacy of existence by considering the univocality of the notion of existence in regards to beings.[112] According to Sadr al-Din-Shirazi, when it is said that a particular tree exists, the word 'exists' is used in the same sense as when it is said that a particular person exists or even that God exists. In other words, the notion of existence is applied to every existent thing in the same sense. For further clarification consider the following argument. Contradictory to the notion of existence is non-existence and things either exist or they do not (i.e. they are either existent or non-existent) and there is no middle ground. Things cannot be both existent and non-existent at the same time because such a proposition is a conjunction of contradictories and therefore impossible to be true. Negating existence and non-existence from things is also impossible because such a proposition is a negation of contradictories which results in the conjunction of contradictories.[113]

---

descriptive mental representation and sense (sense in the way Gottlobe Frege used it) of the essence of an object.

[112]Yazdi, "The Principles of Epistemology in Islamic Philosophy: Knowledge by Presence," 25-26.

[113]Negation of contradictories results in the conjunction of contradictories. If existence is negated in regards to something, that means that non-existence is

Therefore things can either be existent or non-existent and there is no middle ground.[114]

Previous to Sadr Din Shirazi Muslim philosophers distinguished things from each other in terms of their quiddity. Sadr Din Shirazi, on the other hand, despite recognising the fact that in the mental mode of existence (that is in an intelligent being's mind) things are distinguished as such (i.e. in terms of their essence), in reality it is their existence that is principal and not what the mind knows of that existence and hence it has to be their existence that distinguishes them from each other.[115]

Hence, Sadr Din Shirazi rejected the notion that when contingency was proven for an entity, it was proven in regards to the entity's quiddity. He argued that it can never be the case that a contingent entity's quiddity is what is brought into existence because the quiddity is always conceived as

affirmed for it and if non-existence is negated then existence is affirmed, hence if both existence and non-existence is negated then both existence and non-existence is affirmed for something and such a proposition is conjunction of contradictories.

[114]The discussions relating to non-existent concepts such as the golden mountain does not raise any problems for what has just been mentioned because in Islamic philosophy in general and Sadr Din Shirazi's philosophy in particular, concepts are regarded to have mental existence, that is to say they have existence insofar as they are in the mind, since the mind has existence.

[115]A brief note should be added here to clarify this issue further for anyone who might not be familiar with such discussion in Islamic Philosophy. The idea being described here is that what the mind knows of an object is not its external existence but the limitations of that existence. For example, when the mind perceives fire it is not fire that is existent in the mind as it is the case that what is in the mind does not have the same effect as the fire, for example burning. Hence, it is the quiddity of the fire that exists in the mind while the actual fire exists outside of the mind. This is a matter that can be discussed in a variety of philosophical fields including the philosophy of mind and epistemology but that would have to be left for its appropriate place.

equidistant[116] between existence and non-existence. Since existence is principal, then, when contingency is proven for an entity it is proven in regards to its whole reality (which Sadr Din Shirazi equated with dependence).

Sadr Din Shirazi asks: if existence is applied to everything with the same meaning and it is existence which is principal then how can one thing be distinguished from another and what do quiddities represent? Sadr Din Shirazi borrows a concept from the illuminationist philosophy of Sohrawardi to solve this question.

Sohrawardi introduced a notion of 'difference' to Islamic philosophy based on intensification or severity. Using the concept of light Sohrawardi asserts that there is a sort of difference in what things have in common. Light is distinguished from another light not by anything external to the notion of light but by the intensity (or severity) and weakness of the light (or as Sohrawardi labels it by perfection and deficiency).[117] Sadr al-Din Shirazi uses the same principle (i.e. difference in what things have in common) except he replaces the notion of light with that of existence. Hence, according to Sadr al-Din Shirazi existence is sheer existence and therefore existent things are distinguished from each other only through the severity or weakness of their existence (in a sense the notion of the

---

[116]Quiddity is the mental representation of an object's essence and if the object is a contingent object (that is that its existence depends on another and hence can either exist or not exist) then its essence is 'conceived' as being equidistant between existence and non-existence. However, in reality, the object (and its essence) either exists or does not exist and cannot be equidistant towards existence and non-existence.

[117]Suhrawardi, "The Philosophy of Illumination," 85-104.

intensity of existent things is similar to Spinoza's claim of more beings having more attributes). As a result, there is only one existence but beings are distinguished from each other through their place on "gradation of existence". Depending on their severity in this gradation, their limitations are defined. Quiddities (or essences/definitions) are concepts which are abstracted from the limitation of existent beings and it is not the case that the notion of existence is abstracted from quiddities (for example, corporeality is abstracted from a corporeal object because of the limitation it has in terms of existence).

After arguing for the existence of the Necessary Being Sadr Din-Shirazi goes on to explain the relation between contingent beings and the Necessary Being in this gradation of existence:

> All existences that take contingency as their logical modality, and all realities which are related and belong to the Other, are to be considered as different values (i'tabaaraat) and different features of the existence of the Necessary Being. They are rays and shadows of the same Self-Substantive Light. These shadows are, from the stand point of their individuation (huwiyyah), far from being independent. It is impossible even to conceive of them as unrelated and independent entities. This is because 'subordination' and being 'owned by' the Other, as well as need and dependence on the other, are the whole constitution of their reality. It is not however true to suppose that they are something in their essence liable to the occurrences of being related to and owned by the Other, and thus dependent upon the Other; not at all. But rather, the only conceivable truth of their reality is to describe them as a pure 'dependence' on the Other, not even something dependent

on the other. Thus understood, they have no reality in themselves conceivable by our intellectual power other than to be mere subjections and subordinations of One Reality. From this it becomes clear that there is nothing in the world of reality but one single Reality. Anything else other than this counts for nothing but a manifestation, an exhibition, a perspective, a specific manner, a ray of light, a shadow of luminosity and a visage of the endless profundity of this One Reality.[118]

For Sadr al-Din Shirazi, the existence of a contingent being is its mere dependence on the Necessary Being. For further clarification consider contingent beings as prepositional notions or phrases. A preposition is a notion which on its own has no meaning. Such a notion can only be meaningful when its relation to a noun is considered. Hence, when a prepositional notion has meaning, its meaning is the very dependence on a nounal notion. Similar to the relationship between a prepositional notion and the noun which gives it meaning, the mere existence of a contingent being is defined and conceived as dependence on the Necessary Being.[119]

It was from such a philosophical viewpoint, also known as the theory of emanation that the theory of 'Unity of Existence' was originated. Among the English books that have explained the theory of emanation and the concept of unity of existence is the book written by Mehdi Ha'eri Yazdi,

---

[118]Sadr Al-Din Shirazi,. "Kitab al-Asfaar," Vol. 1, 45. Cited in Yazdi, "The Principles of Epistemology in Islamic Philosophy: Knowledge by Presence," 123-124.

[119]Yazdi, "The Principles of Epistemology in Islamic Philosophy: Knowledge by Presence," 124-125.

titled *The Principles of Epistemology in Islamic Philosophy: Knowledge by Presence.* Yazdi takes up the discussion on the theory of emanation and unity of existence in chapter eight of his book when discussing Mysticism in the system of emanation. According to the system of emanation, The First Principle (or First Cause) has created the world (or all the worlds) and entities that reside in them with a single act of emanation. All effects which follow from the First Principle are a single manifestation of this Independent Being. The effects are like a ray of light that has been reflected in a mirror, it is a reflection of the face of the first principle. Without the light there is no reflection.

> An image which appears in a mirror is a mirror by virtue of its essence. According to simple mindsets, glass and other physical parts constitute the mirror; however, in the *'irfan* (Gnosticism) of the wayfarer to the unseen, mirror is nothing but the illustrated visage.[120]

The First Principle himself is simple and indivisible and therefore his action is indivisible, hence the multiplicity of his creation is not due to the multiplicity of his action but due to the nature of the creation.[121] But, in the system of emanation there is no existential void between the First Principle and the entirety of his chain of causes, a notion similar to Spinoza's proposition that there is no causal void between the substance

---

[120]Amuli, "A Commentary on Theistic Arguments," 149.

[121]Yazdi, "The Principles of Epistemology in Islamic Philosophy: Knowledge by Presence," 116-118.

and the infinite modifications which are further down the chain of causality. Yazdi describes this unmediated connection between the First Principle and the chain of causes that follows as thus:

> This indicates that there is an unbroken vertical line connecting all the multitude of emanation to its First Principle in a strictly existential unity. There are also horizontal linkages along which things are to be regarded as different from one another and characterised by multiplicity in rank, in essence, in species, and in individuation.[122]

Thus is unity of existence. Yazdi illustrates the emantionist[123] theory's relation between the First Principle and its effect in the following diagram:

---

[122]Yazdi, "The Principles of Epistemology in Islamic Philosophy: Knowledge by Presence," 125.

[123]Islamic emanationism has various different branches all of which have originated among other things, mainly from two main sources of ancient Persian philosophies of lights and Greek emanationist theories. Although the origin of Islamic emanationist theories comes from these two main sources, it has far advanced both kinds of philosophies through more than a thousand years of philosophizing. It has to be pointed out that in Arabic and Persian phraseology Islamic emanationist theories are not referred to simply as 'emanationism' and are categorized under the type of emanationism they represent, such as the *Falsafeye Ishraaq*, which can be translated as Illuminative Philosophy, *Falsafeye Mota'lliya*, which is the Sadr Al-Din Shirazi's philosophical school of thought, and so on. Many of these philosophical schools are not unique solely based on their theories of the One and its emanation; they also include theories regarding ontology, metaphysics, epistemology, logic and other philosophical concepts. The term emanationism is used here in order to keep to: 1) indicate the emanationist nature of the philosophy and 2) use the common term which is usually used in English description of such philosophical thoughts.

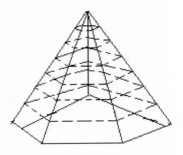

Diagram 1

In Diagram 1, the source of the existence of contingent beings has been compared, by analogy, to a ray of light that flashes out from its main source, the vertical line of existence being united with the First Principle's existence.   All contingent beings are existentially united with the Necessary Being.   Multiplicities are due to the horizontal lines of emanation. In this one reality, beings are distinguished from each other in two ways depending on whether the distinction is being made in terms of the vertical line of emanation or the horizontal one.   Hence, beings are either distinguished from each other through their rank in the vertical line of existence or through their essences, species, etc, in the horizontal line of emanation.

With the aforementioned theory the proponents of the unity of existence claim a sort of pantheism that is significantly different than that of Spinoza.

It is important to mention that the theory of unity of existence is not limited to what has been stated here and there are various different versions with significantly different principles. There is another version of the theory of the unity of existence which states that there is only one reality, one Necessary Being, no gradation, no differentiation; it is only the limited mind which differentiates between the different quiddities that it conceives. This version states that to claim that existence is brought into existence is absurd because that would mean that existence could have not existed (i.e., it could have been non-existence) and such a proposition is contradictory. Hence, existence is necessarily existence and the existence of all existent objects is also necessarily existence. Adding to the aforementioned premise the proposition that existence is sheer and undifferentiated, it can be concluded that in reality there is only one single existence.[124]

Criticism and Evaluation

Despite the fact that the theory of unity of existence (when presented in full) withstands many of the criticisms that apply to the pantheism proposed in the *Ethics* (for example, in regard to proving the existence of the Necessary Being, or proving the dependence of contingent beings on the Necessary Being), nevertheless the same criticisms which were put forward against the idea of unity between the necessary and contingent beings apply to this theory as well. The idea that there is any kind of unity between a being that exists necessarily and a being which exists contingently, entails that a being who has necessary existence is one with a being that is contingent. By claiming that contingent beings are only

---

[124]Amuli, "A Commentary on Theistic Arguments," 181-194.

one with the necessary in regards to their existence but not in regards to their reality (which includes according to Sadr al-Din Shirazi the combination of existence and quiddity) does not solve any problems since quiddity is only the mental conception of the limitation of a contingent being's existence. Therefore, there must be a difference in the contingent being's existence even if only related to its intensity. The difference in intensity is what distinguishes the contingent being's existence with the necessary. That is what eventually led to the proponents of the theory of the unity of existence to eliminate the concept of gradation of existence. If there is something other than the existence that defines the reality of contingent beings then it has to be asked where that thing came from. Aristotle's problem of corporeality existing independently to God once again seems to reveal itself. It seems that, that which is other than the existence of a contingent being and therefore not from God exists independently of God. The mirror seems to be an independent entity reflecting the so called visage of God. But if it is claimed that the whole being of the contingent beings is one with the Necessary Being then the contradiction that arises from the union between contingent and necessary existents apply.

As it was mentioned before even Sadr al-Din Shirazi and the proponents of the theory of unity of existence agree that when it is stated that the existence of a contingent being is contingent, contingency describes the reality of the existent being itself. In other words, it is the reality of an impoverished existent being (which includes its existence) itself that is dependent on the Necessary Being for its existence.   Need and dependence is what characterises the reality of the impoverished being.

Therefore when it is asserted that there is union between the existence of the dependent, impoverished and contingent being with the existence of the Necessary and Independent Being then a conjunction of contradictories is claimed, namely conjunction of the necessary with the contingent, dependence with independence and so forth. For this reason even the theory of the unity of existence does not withstand the criticism which was directed towards Spinoza's pantheism.

Nevertheless, it has to be admitted that once a contingent being exists, it is necessarily existent and it is not true that it is non-existent. It has to also be admitted that the Necessary Being is also necessarily existent and it is not true that it is non-existent. Hence, from one perspective, existence is used in the same sense for both the Necessary Being and the contingent being. However, there is difference between a being that exists necessarily and those that exist contingently. In the case of the Necessary Being, it exists independently of any external cause, which means that the Necessary Being is eternal and independent. In the case of the contingent being, it exists through its dependence on the Necessary Being and is finite. Since the existence of something is one with its being, then the Necessary Being is different from the contingent being in terms of its existence and how it exists.

However, there is still the issue that the notion of existence applies to all existent being in the same univocal sense. The univocality of existence that suggests existence applies to both the Necessary and contingent being in the same manner can be explained in a way that asserts the distinction between the existences of the Necessary Being with that of the

Impoverished Beings. What is required is to distinguish the notion of existence from that of the reality of beings.

Even though the notion of existence is applied to all existing things in the same sense, nevertheless it is the 'notion' of existence which is applied to everything in the same sense, not the reality of every being. In other words, the notion of existence when predicated to another notion as extensional predication, informs that there is a notion that is real and it is not a mere figment of imagination. On the other hand, this notion of existence does not give information about the reality of the real thing, only that it is real. Notions of necessity and contingency or independency and dependency indicate that in reality there is a difference between the being that exists necessarily and beings that are contingent. Furthermore, the two contradictory notions also indicate that their difference is in regards to their reality and since their reality is the same as their existence then the distinction between the Necessary Being and a contingent being reveals that the two different realities are not one in regards to their existence.

It is important to point out that the notion of gradation of existence in the sense that would indicate unity between the existences of contingent beings does not have to be rejected. Also because contingent beings are united in their existence, the notion that all contingent beings are actually one effect from the Necessary Being can also be maintained in the theory of unity of existence. But the idea of unity of existence is not plausible in the way presented by Sadr al-Din Shirazi and his proponents.

A final comment should be added discussing the issue of whether matter of facts regarding contingency of entities and change are merely matters of fact from a finite perspective, which, when viewed from an infinite perspective, such matters of fact are no longer facts but mere illusions.

There is no reason to believe that such matter of facts as entities having contingent existence, change and so on are any different from an infinite perspective. As it has already been argued above, it is perfectly plausible (and in fact a logical necessity) to assert that the Necessary Being is infinite and still existentially separate from finite entities. Since it is plausible or even logically necessary for the Necessary Being to be infinite and existentially separate from finite entities there is no reason why finite entities cannot come into existence (i.e., be contingent) and change. Contingency, change and other attributes of finite entities represent the reality of contingent entities and their reality does not change based on whether or not it is viewed from an infinite perspective (if it is possible for a finite entity to have an infinite perspective) as opposed to a finite perspective.   Therefore, it cannot be asserted that being contingent, subject to change and so on, is just illusions of the finite mind without first proving the claim.

Furthermore, the larger problem of the claim that contingency and change in contingent beings are merely mind's finite understanding of the infinite world is the definition given to infinity by such an assertion. In such an assertion, infinity is taken to mean as including everything. However, defining infinity in this way is assuming the truth of pantheism without proving it.   In addition, the definition of infinity as such is a numerical definition of infinity (i.e., it is only infinite if it includes 'everything'), while the infinity of the Necessary Being is not a numerical infinity but that of total independence and necessity of existing. Therefore, because the Necessary Being cannot be united with contingent beings and because the existence of contingent beings is asserted through arguments of change, then it is absurd to claim that the Necessary Being is infinite only if it is existentially united with contingent beings.   Such an assertion only views infinity in terms of an arbitrary number system while the infinity of the Necessary Being is total independence and lack of need.

BIBLIOGRAPHY

Allison, Henry, E. *Benedictus de Spinoza: An Introduction*. New Haven: Yale University Press, 1987.

Amuli, Jawadi. *A Commentary on Theistic Arguments*. Qom: Ansariyan Publications, 1993.

Curley, E.M. *Spinoza's Metaphysics: An Essay in Interpretation*. Massachusetts: Harvard University Press, 1969.

Hampshire, Stuart. *Spinoza*. London: Faber and Faber.

Moore, Edward. "Plotinus (204-270 C.E.)." The Internet Encyclopedia of Philosophy. <http://www.iep.utm.edu/p/plotinus.htm> (2004)

Spinoza, Benedictus De. *Ethics*, trans. A. Boyle. J.M. Dent & Sons Ltd.

Stace, W. T. *Mysticism and Philosophy*. New York: Jeremy P. Tarcher, 1960.

Suhrawardi. *The Philosophy of Illumination*, Trans. John Walbridge & Hossein Ziai. Utah: Brigham University Press, 1999.

Yazdi, Mehdi, Ha'iri. *The Principles of Epistemology in Islamic Philosophy: Knowledge by Presence*. New York: State University of New York Press, 1992.

Made in the USA
Coppell, TX
11 October 2021